BEFORE
the Dissertation

A Textual Mentor for Doctoral Students
at Early Stages of a Research Project

Christine Pearson Casanave

Foreword by John M. Swales

Ann Arbor

University of Michigan Press

♾ Printed on acid-free paper

ISBN-13: 978-0-472-03600-4

2017   2016   2015   2014   4   3   2   1

Dedication

I dedicate this book to all the doctoral students I have worked with, who have taught me so much.

Acknowledgments

Special thanks to Youngjoo Yi and Robert Kohls, who provided insightful comments and suggestions on the entire manuscript. The book is much improved thanks to you. I am also grateful to the following people for their comments on earlier drafts or pieces of the book and for their support and encouragement along the way: Hanako Okada, Stephanie Vandrick, Yongyan Li, Merrill Swain, Shirley Laska, Monte Piliawsky, and the anonymous reviewers at University of Michigan Press. As always, I am especially grateful to Kelly Sippell, who has supported my sometimes quirky projects and writing styles over the years. Without her encouragement, this book would not have been possible.

Foreword by John M. Swales

Thirty years ago I was asked to give a paper on ESP at a small, invitational conference held at the University of London to celebrate the first half-century of The British Council. Those invited to speak were requested "to take a bold stand with regard to future developments." The eventual title of my paper was "ESP: The Heart of the Matter or the End of the Affair." As readers may recognize, this title invokes two famous novels by Graham Greene, partly because Greene's published career began at about the same time as the founding of the council. As for that "bold stand," I put forward two main proposals. The first was that English for Academic Purposes (EAP) should move beyond its traditional focus on service courses for undergraduates (with a concomitant attention to genres such as textbooks, lectures and lab reports) and become more involved in graduate education and research English. This, I argued, would provide both a reinvigorating challenge and also help to raise the status of EAP units within their university settings. Second, I suggested that a narrow focus on texts—on attention to purely textual matter—should be widened to include more study on the processes by means of which those texts are conceived, generated, and negotiated. In effect, a plea for case studies of an ethnographical character. This second proposal led me to conclude:

> As for my title and its original disjunctive question, readers who have followed me so far will recognize that what I should have written was: ESP—The End of the Matter but the Heart of the Affair.

I have not mentioned this 1985 paper in order to revive the embers of a moribund fire—it appears to have received a single citation in the last six years! Rather, it serves to show that the first of my suggestions has been validated and widely implemented by later developments, while the second has been only partly so. Although there have been important contributions to our understanding of how graduate students and junior researchers become acculturated into their disciplinary matrices by the likes of Christine Pearson Casanave, John Flowerdew, Roz Ivanič, Theresa Lillis, Paul Prior, and Christine Tardy, there is still a perception in some quarters that EAP remains "too textual" in its orientation, particularly with regard to published articles (Lillis & Scott, 2007). Further, most of these studies have targeted, in diverse ways, success and failure in academic writing.

In her new book entitled *Before the Dissertation*, Christine Pearson Casanave explores a rather different set of educational circumstances and does so by deliberately shifting the emphasis away from writing to thinking, reading, and feeling. The book is designed for doctoral students as they attempt to transition from taking courses to beginning to conduct independent research. This can indeed be a perilous time that tends to involve different cognitive, emotional and interpersonal demands and pressures from those of coursework; indeed, according to the available studies, as many as 40-50 percent of entering doctoral students fail to finish—a statistic that universities do not typically shout from the rooftops. The primary audience consists of students in the social sciences, broadly conceived to include education and intercultural studies, and wears its scholarship lightly (despite an impressive bibliography). The style is personal, uncluttered, and informal; as a result, the book is highly readable.

Before the Dissertation consists of an introduction followed by nine chapters. All these chapters start with a myth, such as "Theory plays an essential and elevated role in doctoral work," which is then deconstructed, followed by various kinds of advice and suggestion much enlivened by rich case study extracts. Some of these stories recount episodes from Dr. Casanave's own experiences as a doctoral student, but most are drawn from her own graduate students and from published narratives. Although the volume will prove very useful for all doctoral students in their early and middle years in social science programs, students who have English as an additional language and/or who have earned their first degrees outside the United States may perhaps benefit the most. For a single example, Chapter 7, "Finding Advisers-Supervisors and Mentors," addresses many of the misunderstandings that can arise between the parties, including those that occur because international students are not always as proactive as they might be. While my own experience as an adviser certainly contains instances of international students who over-relied on being told what to do, I vividly remember one exception. After our meetings, a student from South Asia always used to write me a memo outlining what we had agreed needed to be done, but also including a section stating what *she did not need to do*. Later, if I suggested she that might look at something else, she would produce the relevant memo and say "Look, you said I needn't do this." She got her PhD in under five years and is now Dean of Graduate Studies at a leading private university in her home country.

Although the volume will help many students avoid becoming isolated from their departments or alienated from their programs, it will also be valuable for advisers as well. Out of many instances of things that I have insufficiently thought about was this one: "I know I have learned a great deal from my own doctoral students, but I fear I have not let them know often enough how much they have taught me" (p. 109). So, for all these reasons, I am sure that *Before the Dissertation* will and should be widely adopted.

References

Lillis, T., & Scott, M. (2007). Defining academic literacies research: Issues of epistemology, ideology and strategy. *Journal of Applied Linguistics*, *4*, 5–32.

Swales, J. M. (1985). ESP—The heart of the matter or the end of the affair. In R. Quirk & H. G. Widdowson (Eds.), *English in the world: Teaching and learning the language and literatures* (pp. 212–223). Cambridge, U.K.: Cambridge University Press.

Contents

Introduction

When David Sternberg (1981) wrote his still-engaging if occasionally outdated (and scary!) book on how to survive a doctoral dissertation, he claimed that no how-to books of the type he was writing existed. Today, dozens of books now aim to help students prepare and write doctoral proposals and dissertations (do a google search!). So why offer a book on the doctoral dissertation journey to a market that is already flooded with how-to-write-proposals-and-dissertations books, including ones that focus on quantitative, qualitative, and mixed-methods inquiry in the social sciences? I guess because this book is *not* another one of those, in that it is not a how-to-write book or even a how-to-do-research book.

Instead, *Before the Dissertation* concerns issues to consider *before* students start writing, indeed before they commit to a major high-stakes dissertation project, whether qualitative or quantitative or something in between. It is especially relevant for students who wish to do projects that involve a lengthy research period (which can add to stress), and that also involve reading, data collection, and writing in more than one language. From the earliest stages of doctoral work, even before the proposal stage, and during intermediate stages of preparation for a project as well, there are things to think about and discuss with friends, family, and advisers such as: Why do you want to pursue a doctoral degree? Do you fully understand what you are getting into? How will you manage to develop an appropriate topic? What will your role be in your project and what languages will you use with multilingual participants? How might you engage with reading, people, and personal writing at early stages in ways that will contribute to your project's development? How much attention should you pay to quality-of-life issues?

In all these senses, this book starts well before other books do and stops where they begin. Still, many existing books touch on the issues in *Before the Dissertation*, so there is nothing radically new here—just an expansion of what tends to be underdiscussed in the proposal-dissertation writing guidebooks and an organic approach rather than a linear and prescriptive one.

☞ Overview of *Before the Dissertation*

This book consists of nine short chapters that for the most part can be read in any order. Some of the main points of the book are repeated in some of the chapters, for those readers who read selectively. However, the first several chapters discuss some important preliminary issues that might best be considered first, such as reasons for students' decision to begin doctoral study in the first place and quality-of-life concerns. Each chapter begins with a common myth about advanced academic work that I hope to quickly dispel. The chapters then lay out some issues and offer some examples (stories) from my work with students, from my own experiences, or from existing literature on early doctoral study. The chapters pose questions that connect issues directly with individual readers so as to help them make sensible decisions about their doctoral work. A summary of main points and suggestions for discussion and reflection are offered at the end of each chapter.

The book could be used in graduate classes on issues in doctoral study, most usefully earlier rather than later in the program of study, such as introduction to graduate study or early seminars on dissertation planning. It lends itself well to intense and personal discussion among class members and encourages peer support as well as regular interaction with professors and advisers. It could also be a companion (a "textual mentor"; see the definition in Chapter 1) to individual students who, on their own, wish to reflect on their decision to pursue doctoral studies and on what might lie ahead for them in the coming several years of work on a doctoral project. It will accompany all readers in their early stages of thinking, reading, discussing, exploratory and reflective writing, and decision-making. The style of the book is intended to be personal and engaging, free of jargon and unnecessary terminology, and respectful of mature L1, L2, and EAL (first language, second language, English as an additional language) readers of English. I hope that my personal style will help keep all of us from taking ourselves too seriously. (Seriously—you will not die if you don't finish a doctoral dissertation.)

☞ The Audience for This Book

Before the Dissertation speaks to an audience in the social sciences, but in particular to one that I am especially interested in and familiar with: doctoral students who have experience with and interest in international and multilingual students as well as native English–speaking students in diverse settings who wish to investigate topics in (second) language and multicultural-transcultural education. Much of this research is conducted in various linguistic and cultural contexts and makes use of more than one language for data collection, analysis, and writing—a focus not apparent in most guide books. Nevertheless, although appropriate for use in English-dominant doctoral programs throughout the world, some of my points will pertain more closely to students in the North American educational system than to ones, for example, in the British system. Some years of course work and planning typify the former, but not the latter. It is likely that many of the issues I discuss are indeed experienced by graduate students in the British-style system, but at the master's level stage, before they have actually begun a doctoral program, as well as early in their doctoral programs. Although many of my resources concerning advising and supervising of doctoral students are from U.K.-system authors, my primary focus will be on the North American context. The decisions for students are the same: Why am I doing a doctoral program? What kind of research project will possibly sustain me for several years? What is the role of the doctoral adviser-supervisor and how can I best manage this relationship?

The main audience for this book is thus doctoral students who are first or second/additional users of English, who are interested in pursuing topics in one of the social sciences (including education and multilingual inquiry), and who may just be finishing course work in an English-dominant university and are wondering what might happen next. Sternberg (1981) long ago pointed out what is still true today (see Lovitts, 2005): The dissertation phase of a doctoral program is really a second, different program from the course work stage. Students nearing the end of course work (in the North American system) might have little idea how they will get through the very different dissertation stage. I think it is not much easier for students in the British system who need to start thinking about their projects without the years of required course work to ease them into a project. So, *Before the Dissertation* will be a good companion for students who feel a bit lost and fit the following descriptions: those who wonder if they made the right decision to pursue a doctoral degree; who have little sense of what a good research topic for them will be; who believe that everyone else around them already knows how to do research and write in flawless academic English and that they were admitted to their program by mistake; or who are overwhelmed by pressures and obligations in their lives that have nothing to do with doctoral work. I hope to convince such readers that they are in good company. (Out of curiosity, consider asking your professors and adviser(s) what *they* went through in completing their doctoral degrees.)

But what if you are a master's-level student at this stage? It is also possible that, even though this book is written mainly for doctoral students, master's students who are required to write a thesis in order to graduate will also benefit from reading it. Moreover, for those master's students who are considering continuing to study at the doctoral level, *Before the Dissertation* might provide some advanced information (warning?) about what lies ahead. A decision to pursue a doctoral degree should not be made lightly. It hardly makes sense to realize several years into a degree program that this was not really what you wanted to spend your time, money, and effort on (attrition rates in doctoral programs are depressingly high; see Golde, 2000, 2005).

Other important readers will be doctoral instructors, advisers, and mentors, who may find that *Before the Dissertation* offers some insights into what some doctoral students go through in the months, or even years, before they write their proposals and actually start their doctoral research and begin communicating with their advisers. These insights may inspire faculty to connect with graduate students in expanded ways and also to begin discussing issues in dissertation work with them earlier rather than later. The book may also help instructors and advisers understand the kinds of obstacles faced by some students that tend to impede or halt their progress. If, on the other hand, advisers take a hands-off approach, in which they want to see a student only when that student has a dissertation chapter drafted and ready to be critiqued, then this book probably goes beyond what they believe their job should be. (Such advisers may not distinguish between a hands-on approach and hand-holding, but they are not the same.) There are always dilemmas about how involved advisers need to be in students' lives and work, but the literature on supervising generally concludes that closer, more regular attention pays off pragmatically and psychologically (Delamont, Parry, & Atkinson, 1998; Lee, 2007; Lunsford, 2012; Meloy, 1994; Zhao, Golde, & McCormick, 2007).

Finally, it is possible that students who are pursuing English-dominant doctoral degrees in their second languages (English as an L2 or additional language) might find the mentorship in *Before the Dissertation* especially comforting, although the ideas and issues apply to all doctoral students. As Paltridge and Starfield (2007) discussed in their book for supervisors, international students who use English as a second language might be unfamiliar with some of the unwritten and often unspoken expectations in U.S.- or U.K.-style doctoral programs. For instance, if students expect to be told what to do every step of the way, to be assigned a topic, to be handed a full reading list without needing to search for their own literature, and to receive (rather than pro-actively negotiate) detailed and prescriptive advice, they will likely be disappointed. In the social sciences, unlike in some of the hard sciences, they will probably be working on a topic of their choosing (in consultation with an adviser) rather than on a team project under the umbrella guidance of a main faculty member who has gotten grant money. It will be up to individual students to seek help, to teach their adviser(s) about themselves, their home cultures, and their hopes and expectations, and to instigate change if they are not satisfied (cf. Fujioka, 2008).

But whether students are pursuing a doctoral degree in English as an additional language or English as a first or dominant language, *Before the Dissertation* will provide them with many things to think about before they actually start writing a proposal or commit to doctoral research. Some things are good to think about before it's too late—in other words, before energy, peace of mind, and bank accounts are depleted. The decision to pursue a doctoral degree needs to be the right one.

⌒ Chapter Summaries

Chapter 1 is a foundational chapter in that it explains the rationale for the book, defines what I mean by "textual mentor," and reviews some of the common problems that prospective dissertation writers face. It stresses the importance of doing sufficient homework, leg work, head work, and heart work before committing to a doctoral journey.

Chapter 2 is a second foundational chapter. Just as there are many reasons for pursuing a doctoral degree (both external and internal incentives), there are also reasons not to do so, or reasons to adjust the timing of students' commitment. Although it seems common sense, prospective dissertation writers might not know the specific requirements and demands at their university; it pays to ask earlier rather than later. This chapter also addresses questions about conducting projects involving more than one language. Importantly, it emphasizes quality-of-life issues having to do with health, relationships, and balance—topics rarely discussed in dissertation guide books. In general, it asks a lot of questions that would be wise for students to consider before they make a final commitment.

Chapter 3 discusses several types of writing that usefully help shape a project at its early stages and that aid planning, decision-making, and record-keeping. These include research memos, dissertation journals, field notes, personal journals, and "academic letters." Such writing can liberate novice researchers from fear of being judged harshly by others and can provide an emotional outlet (something essential) because this kind of personal writing can be written in any way the writers wish, with impunity.

Chapter 4 asks where ideas come from and explores initial thoughts on topics that are and are not appropriate for a major book-length research project. One of the points of this chapter is that a topic that sustains interest, curiosity, and commitment over time (including for publications that come post-dissertation) must come from the heart (personal experience, philosophy of teaching and learning, current work issues) and yet be capable of connecting with others (including a faculty adviser) and with literature in the field. It also addresses issues of access to research sites and securing consent of participants, both of which are important to think about at the early topic-development stage.

Chapter 5 is devoted to reading and discusses the role of reading in topic development and knowledge building. Some disagreement exists as to how steeped in reading students need to be at early stages of dissertation work and how central the literature review is at these early stages, so I present my pro-reading stance as one of several views. I also include in this chapter some early suggestions and cautions about keeping track of and organizing readings and of reflecting on them in reading response journals.

Chapter 6 reviews what it means to "think theoretically and conceptually." Written for people who fear terms like *theory* and are confused by the requirement that they provide a theoretical or conceptual framework for their research project, the chapter untangles some of the mysteries of abstract thinking and offers some strategies for conceptual framing that are useful to think about as a project develops.

Chapter 7 presents some issues concerning finding advisers and mentors and beginning to think way down the line about committee members. The stance I take in this chapter is that decisions about who to work with, how to work with them, and how to construct a committee are political, psychological, and emotional as well as pragmatic. Such decisions are also negotiable. Prospective dissertation writers need to take a proactive stance in forging and managing these relationships.

Chapter 8 suggests another important source of help in shaping a project and making decisions, that of supportive people such as study groups, friends, and colleagues-classmates. Even one or two trusted people can form a reciprocal mentoring relationship that will last over time. This kind of support is different from that provided by professors and advisers (see Chapter 7).

In Chapter 9 I return to the question of topic, and how readings, writings, and supportive discussions and exchanges can help doctoral students develop and refine their topics. Once a topic has been refined, students should be ready to commit seriously to their projects (focused reading, dissertation proposals, data collection, analysis, early writing).

Chapter 1

Foundational Issues

┌─ **MYTH #1** ─────────────────────────────────┐

Students who don't finish their doctoral program will be considered failures.

> This is simply not true. There are many good reasons for pushing yourself to finish a doctoral degree and many good reasons for leaving, or not even starting, a program. A doctoral degree is not necessarily required for a successful career or sense of personal fulfillment in life.

└───┘

As I noted in the Introduction, the hardest part of the doctoral dissertation process, I think, confronts us before the dissertation writing begins. Once you are ready to begin writing the actual doctoral thesis, most of the hard work is done and many of the confusions and anxieties and complications have been resolved or at least mitigated. So this book is not about dissertation writing.

For one thing, I am not a first-hand expert on dissertation writing. I have written only one in my life, like other doctoral graduates. My experiences with doctoral students are also not widespread or lengthy. They have taken place mainly at an American university campus in Japan since 2004, where I have taught and advised doctoral students from the early stages of work on their qualitative dissertations in second language education through to the final defense. I had discovered in my own doctoral journey the time-consuming, complex, and intriguing nature of qualitative inquiry, and these complexities certainly have surfaced in students' projects. But in Japan I became aware of the additional complications that arise from collecting data in one language and writing a dissertation in another, the near-impossibility of devoting full time to dissertation work when students have full-time jobs and families, the difficulties and hazards of selecting appropriate topics in their very constrained situations (e.g., topics that were complex and interesting, sustainable long-term, amenable to workable methods and to book-length treatment), and the frustrations in finding compatible advisers. I began watching students more closely, reading what I could find, and wondering how any of them made it through to the end. Then, as I began to read more about doctoral study, I realized that doctoral students throughout the social sciences (i.e., disciplines that study people and their activities), who do diverse kinds of projects using various methods, face similar issues as they approach the dissertation writing stage.

You might still be at the very beginning of your doctoral studies, and like many of us, feel that you were admitted to your program by mistake (the "fraud" syndrome; McIntosh, 1989). But if you have managed or are determined to work through this anxiety, you might be nearing the point in your doctoral studies where you need to make the transition soon to the Big D (dissertation, in the U.S. system, and thesis, in the British system). If so, you have both my admiration and my sympathies. This stage, the most important in your doctoral career, could either be one of the most interesting and stimulating periods in your life or a journey into hell. For most of us who managed to complete this journey, it was a mix—in my case, a lot of the former and a bit too much of the latter. This small book is intended to get you off to a good start on this journey by helping raise your awareness about what you are getting yourself into and by helping you make sensible decisions early in the process.

However, please stop reading right now if you are expecting another book on how to write a dissertation. As I mentioned in the Introduction, this is not a how-to-write book. It might better be described as a how-to-think-before-you-write book and a what-emotions-to-expect book. I wish I could do more, such as provide some recipes for how to have fun on your dissertation journey. However, in my long career, I have rarely heard the doctoral dissertation journey described as fun. Just as I cannot promise any recipes for writing, I cannot promise any recipes for fun in this book, although I will certainly make a case for keeping a (black) sense of humor. (A good laugh can release a lot of stress.) Rather than being described as fun, more often the journey is characterized as difficult, isolating, impossible, torturous, depressing, boring, intimidating, endless, but also challenging, fascinating, absorbing, and life-changing. Some of those responses and emotions are pretty much guaranteed.

Another guarantee I can make is found in an important message running through *Before the Dissertation*: You are not alone. Not only are there thousands like you, and thousands who made the dissertation journey before you, including your own professors, but you also now have a small book to keep you company: a "textual mentor."

⌢ The Concept of a "Textual Mentor"

The subtitle of *Before the Dissertation* refers to this book as a "textual mentor." Stephanie Vandrick and I first used this term in our 2003 edited book, *Writing for Scholarly Publication* (Casanave & Vandrick,

2003). By this term, we wished to suggest that the chapters in that book were intended to make personal, supportive, informative, and insightful connections with readers who are trying to write for publication and who might be frustrated or confused about what is involved. This stance differs from that of a prescriptive how-to approach because a mentor does not simply tell you what to do. (A recipe can do that.) Rather than relying on a "you should do xyz" approach, a mentor makes both emotional and pragmatic connections with a mentee and is concerned with a mentee's well-being as well as with the tasks and activities (in the case of the present book) of a doctoral project (Casanave & Li, 2012; Creighton, Creighton, & Parks, 2010; Lunsford, 2012). A mentor works with others from a stance of caring (Noddings, 2003) and is sustained by the responses of the ones who are mentored (Casanave & Li, 2012). I have written this book from a stance of caring, and I hope I will be sustained by responses from readers who find that it offers them hope and encouragement, in spite of difficulties that all dissertation writers face.

Common Problems Faced by Prospective Dissertation Writers

Story: My own story of dropping one project and starting over

Many years ago I wrote a doctoral qualifying paper, and designed and carried out a sort of pilot project as I was preparing to write a dissertation proposal. I worked on this topic, in the area of second language reading, for a year, but something wasn't working. I am still not sure why the project did not, could not, would not evolve into a dissertation. I do know that I was unsure what I was getting myself into, that I did not feel inspired and excited, that I was not writing reflective journals to try to work through my confusions, and that one of my professors was just introducing me to issues in writing research that seemed more promising. I also know that I was not encouraged by classmates and professors to seek a topic of personal importance to me, such as my own experiences learning to write in graduate school. Once I realized that my research really needed to be, at some level, about myself, my project took off. How does it happen, I wondered, that someone can start a doctoral program as one kind of person (in my case an ESL teacher interested in practice) and, after years of nonstop reading and writing, walk out the university door as another kind of person (in my case a researcher interested in the transformative nature of graduate-level academic literacy practices)? But during the PhD journey, my ESL identity disappeared or at least lost focus. I no longer knew what to put on a business card except "student." And I was, relatively speaking, a very old student, and the label felt uncomfortable.

When I look back on this story now, I am struck by how familiar it sounds. Many years after completing my degree and after working in recent years with doctoral students who have to write dissertations (and watching some of them disappear, never to finish), I realize that a lot of students have started a doctoral program mid-career with a strong teacher identity and then floundered about (great metaphor!), not quite knowing what to expect after course work when they had to become real researchers. This is partly because the dissertation stage of a doctoral program is really a different program from course work, for which few of us are prepared no matter how well we did in the course work stage (Sternberg, 1981). As I did, many students I have known searched about for an appropriate research topic and compatible methodology and wondered where and how to get help from knowledgeable others.

So in recent years I have become aware of the need for resources that might help students think through their dissertation journeys at an earlier stage than actual proposal and dissertation writing—before they have committed their heart, souls, and bank accounts to this second long stage of the doctoral program. Of course a committed and engaged adviser will serve the same function as a think-along book. But often there are not enough advisers to go around, or the advisers do not see their roles as ones of think-along partners at early stages, preferring instead to wait to see some actual writing from students, or they don't know how to give up their authoritarian roles of telling students what to do rather than thinking along with them, or there isn't good chemistry between adviser and student, or they simply can't make time in their busy schedules.

Challenges and issues, in other words, abound, ones that come before and go beyond the actual writing of a thesis or dissertation (Paltridge & Woodrow, 2012). Two of the most difficult challenges I've noticed are topic choice and isolation. Dissertation topics in the social sciences can be particularly hard to come by. In many social sciences, students' doctoral projects are individually designed and are not part of the work of research teams, as is common in the natural sciences. Social science students, therefore, are pretty much on their own when it comes to constructing and carrying out a feasible doctoral research project without ever having done this kind of work before. Writing a course paper cannot be compared to the doctoral project. Moreover, in the case of my students in Japan (a mix of native- and nonnative speakers of English), once they have finished course work, they scatter and work in relative isolation, no longer needing to commute from all over a large metropolitan area in Japan to the commuter campus buildings in Tokyo or Osaka. Monthly study groups would be ideal, but most students I have worked with usually could not make the time to meet because travel times were too long, and work obligations even on weekends were too pressing. Weekends, if there was any free time, were devoted to family matters. Post–course work isolation is endemic and is a common phenomenon elsewhere too. I felt it in my own doctoral work long ago.

Hoping not to discourage dissertation writers from reading further, I present here some specific problems that are steeped in the realities of doctoral work. I'll talk about these issues and more in various chapters throughout the book.

1. In my experience, one problem seems to be that some students are uncertain as to why—in mid-career oftentimes—they are pursuing a doctoral degree. Some of my students already have tenured jobs teaching in Japan and are quite content with their positions. Why go through the tremendous expense and effort required to complete a doctoral degree? Other students might want the degree in order to advance in their careers, but are not sure whether they need a doctoral degree to do this. And some students just like to study and want to continue the intellectual and social interactions they enjoyed in the their master's programs. The realities of dissertation work can come as a shock in such cases—one of these realities being the extraordinary amount of time it can take to complete this journey (in the United States, six to ten years is common, especially for part-time students). In short, uncertainty as to purpose can prevent students from developing a focused vision for a project that is feasible and that will sustain them over several years. I've known students who fit all these descriptions.

2. Another problem primarily centers on the difficulty some students have in developing a research-oriented topic that is appropriate for a book-length project. As is the case for nearly everyone who has done a doctoral dissertation, we do this high-stakes project once in a lifetime. None of us has experienced doing such a project before we actually

have to do it—people don't write "practice" dissertations; pilot studies are not the same as the real thing. So, as astonishing as this is in an educational sense, experience is no guide. Some graduates go on to write books, at which point the dissertation experience can usefully inform the book project. Still, most students face this book-length doctoral project for the first and only time in their lives. When one has only written course papers, it is challenging to envision the enormity of such a project. Many ideas for topics that my students have come up with are too limited for a doctoral project, but would make great course papers or even a short master's thesis. The other side of this problem is that some students are overly committed to ideas that are so huge that it would take a decade and a multi-volume book series to do them justice.

3. A third problem that affects some students is the lack of compatible and consistent guidance over the several years of project work (see the tale told by Fujioka, 2008, and also some of the literature on doctoral supervision in the British system such as Delamont, Parry, & Atkinson, 1998; Ives & Rowley, 2005; Kamler & Thomson, 2008; Lee, 2007, 2008; Li & Seale, 2007; Paltridge & Starfield, 2007; Stracke & Kumar, 2010). As I mentioned, doctoral work can be quite isolating once course work is done (as in U.S. universities), or if students are working more or less on their own from the start with one supervisor (as in many U.K.-style universities). Sometimes it is difficult to find an appropriate adviser or supervisor. Then, once hooked up with someone, some students hesitate to change, even if their relationship with the adviser is not working well (e.g., personality clashes, lack of sufficient attention, an adviser's sparse knowledge of the student's topic; conflict of ideas about research paradigms; see Sternberg's [1981] stories of abusive or neglectful advisers

he knew in the U.S. context). The world of doctoral research can thus be quite discouraging or at least confusing if students feel they are alone and there is nowhere to turn for help. Moreover, insensitive critiques from advisers and professors can discourage students from persisting in their efforts. Add to this the psychological burden of guilt: Many students I have known have felt that they are the only ones in their program who are going through serious difficulties, and (in their minds) this must certainly be because they are not as bright, not as accomplished in English, or not as committed and motivated as their classmates. None of that is true, of course. Such comparisons are truly insidious.

4. Finally, for mid-career teachers and professionals who decide to pursue doctoral studies, many unpredictable hurdles can present themselves as taking priority over the doctoral project: health issues, child care, elderly care, financial difficulties, and unrelenting pressures from jobs that students cannot afford to give up (Casanave, 2010a). The university, and advisers, may not know, or care, about these real-life obstacles. Send me drafts of chapters, they say; we'll talk then.

Existing proposal-thesis-dissertation guides (books and articles) on the market do not cover most of the concerns raised in the previous list other than possibly paying them lip-service. Instead, they make the doctoral project seem quite linear and systematic, if not easy. However, the prescriptive advice in published guide books does not always match practical realities (Kamler & Thomson, 2008; Paltridge, 2002). Instead, many of the guide books start at the researching-writing stage and devote little or no attention to topic development, decision-making in early stages, emotional issues, and human relationships. Especially in the second language education field, guidebooks tend to focus

on linguistic and rhetorical issues including: genre, academic
(meta)language, rhetorical organization of the whole and of different sections, citation conventions, and so on (see, for example, the *English in Today's Research World* series of small volumes
by Swales and Feak and their 2012 textbook, and the book for
supervisors by Paltridge and Starfield, 2007). These matters are of
course important, but quite different from the issues that arise in
the months, even years, before the proposal- and thesis-writing
stages. For instance, many how-to books imply that choosing a
topic for dissertation research is fairly straightforward rather than
fraught with danger if students commit too quickly to a topic
that will not suit or sustain them. They also just don't seem to
deal with the early stages of struggle and confusion so common
to some students, particularly those leaning toward complex,
labor-intensive qualitative and multilingual research projects,
other than warning that topic development can take a long time
(see the slightly better coverage in Maxwell, 2005, 2013; Murray
& Beglar, 2009; Silverman & Marvasti, 2008; Sternberg, 1981).

Hence this book: *Before the Dissertation*. Be forewarned: I
won't be giving you any tips on conducting research (see other
books), on writing a proposal (see other books), or on writing
up your research for the full dissertation (see other books). There
will be no templates for research in this book, no grammar or
rhetorical lessons, no advice on stylistic conventions or on citing
and referencing works (see other books). But I will ask you to
consider why you are doing a doctoral degree; where ideas for
major projects come from; why prolonged attention to developing a topic that is right for you is essential; how friends, advisers, and classmates, and good health and sleep can help get you
through; how reading and writing in reflective journals or memos
can help you find your way into and through a project; and why
quality-of-life issues might make the difference between finishing and not finishing.

☞ Pre-Proposal Homework, Leg Work, Head Work, and Heart Work

One of the main messages of this book is how much work there is to do before doctoral students write and submit a dissertation proposal and begin the actual work of the dissertation. Some of this homework involves information–gathering by students about their own universities concerning what is involved procedurally once they have finished course work and what resources (human, textual, technological) are available. Leg work is involved too—determining possible research sites and seeking out and actually talking to possible advisers and mentors who share interests and compatible research approaches. Head work is involved in the many hours of thinking, pondering, mulling, reading, talking, and reflecting that contribute to decisions about a doctoral research project. And finally, heart work cannot be neglected. What intellectual passions and curiosities drive someone to devote several years of an adult life to inquiry, and how can these passions be channeled and nourished? And what connections and relationships to family and friends will sustain students during this period of stresses and strains, and how can energy and time be allocated to these relationships without jeopardizing work on the dissertation project? How can students build and sustain belief and confidence in themselves during a lengthy experience that can leave them feeling intimidated, depressed, confused, and defeated? The dissertation journey is an emotional as well as an intellectual one.

Not everything can be known at the start of a major project of course. Surprises and shifts are inevitable, particularly in qualitative inquiry. But by doing some homework, leg work, head work, and heart work before the dissertation, students are likely to make sensible decisions and to avoid the discouragement that results from being unprepared and overwhelmed.

Summary of Main Points in This Chapter

1. Most doctoral dissertation guides do not deal in depth with issues to be considered before you begin your a dissertation, such as reasons for pursuing a doctoral degree and the realities of committing several years of your life to doing so.

2. Various kinds of homework, leg work, head work, and heart work are important to do before committing yourself to the dissertation stage of your doctoral program.

3. A "textual mentor"—a small book to accompany you on your journey—can provide some advice and solace. But it won't take the place of support from advisers, friends, and family on your intellectual and emotional journey.

Suggestions for Discussion and Reflection

1. What stories have you heard from other people (classmates, graduates, professors, teaching assistants, etc.) about the dissertation process? How do you react to those stories? How do they make you feel about your own case?

2. What fears do you have about embarking on a dissertation project? Where do these fears come from?

3. What proposal- or dissertation-writing guides have you or classmates looked at? What are your feelings about the usefulness of such books at the stage of the doctoral program that you are currently in?

Chapter 2

Things to Consider before Deciding to Pursue a Doctoral Degree

┌─ MYTH #2 ──────────────────────────────────

Students who complete their doctoral programs must certainly be brilliant.

There is no necessary role for brilliance in a doctoral program. Most people who complete doctoral degrees are not brilliant. They are smart, strategic, and tenacious.

└───

If you have read Chapter 1 in this book, you have a preview of some of the problems students encounter on their doctoral program journey, particularly at the dissertation stage. I don't bring these things up to discourage readers, but to offer some things to consider before they get so deeply entrenched that they feel trapped—some realities, as it were, that might prevent some difficulties later.

So in this chapter I'd like to ask some further foundational questions that would be useful to consider early in the doctoral journey, well before dissertation stage. The questions are about why students pursue doctoral degrees, about why a surprisingly large number of students drop out before they finish, about learning what demands and resources there are at particular universities, and about some quality-of-life issues that sneak up on people insidiously.

☞ Some Sensible—and Not So Sensible—Reasons for Pursuing a Doctorate

The most basic question in this chapter asks why you are pursuing a doctoral degree. I did not think about this question much until I started working with a diverse group of doctoral students. My own case had seemed quite clear cut. I was teaching ESL full time, with a master's degree, and was quite content. I was surprised to be let go (laid off, dropped, fired, removed, moved aside?) along with all the other full-time ESL teachers at my school. It was nothing personal apparently—we were all treated equally, our places taken by part-timers and students in the TESOL master's program. We were given a year's notice to start a new life somewhere else. I realized then how much I loved university life, and that I might not be able to continue in this life without a PhD. Scary. I was nearly 40. I decided to go back to school so that later I could seek and secure a job as a university instructor. This long-term goal provided me the tenacity I needed to finish. Plus, I discovered that I liked to study. (Better late than never.)

I met my own doctoral students (a mix of Japanese and non-Japanese) much later, during their course work at the American university campus in Japan where I began teaching part time after 13 years of teaching at a Japanese university. I was interested to learn that there seemed to be as many reasons for pursuing a doctoral degree as there were students. Many of the students I met already had full-time tenured jobs that they had no intention of leaving. For them, the degree seemed unrelated to professional goals. Others had contract positions and wished to get tenured jobs, thinking that the doctoral degree would help. Some had part-time jobs and wished to get anything full time. Some were considering leaving Japan and wanted a diploma in hand for their next career move. Some were middle-aged mid-career women who had families and parents to take care of and no strong financial or career goals. They weren't sure why they were in the program, but it was a wonderful change from their rather enclosed lives.

I recall asking two women (featured in the two stories in Chapter 4) over an adviser-advisee lunch meeting a couple of years ago why they wanted a doctoral degree. They both had ten-ured jobs they were satisfied with. My question was one of mild desperation, because no matter how many times we consulted by email and in person, they couldn't seem to find their way into an appropriate dissertation topic. They weren't sure how to respond at first, and I wondered if they had thought seriously about their enormous commitment of time and money (no fellowships or scholarships at the Japan branch of this American university). Finally, they gave me two quite different answers. One said that she felt quite powerless to make changes at her school, or in the Japanese educational system, as a woman without an advanced degree. The degree would be her way of establishing some power and authority—to have a voice. This made sense. The other waf-fled. She finally said that she thought having a doctoral degree would improve her confidence and her self-image. She is right, but I wondered if this reason was strong enough to carry her through the second half of the program—the dissertation stage. A third case struck me too. This one concerned a woman about my age—mid-60s at the time—who had retired from her full-time job to work on her dissertation, who might not ever work full time again post-doctoral degree, but who simply refused to give up something she had started and that years before she had promised her bewildered mother that she would finish. As I draft this chapter, she is still trying, in year 10, and her mother has since passed away. Now that is tenacity.

So some students have strong clear professional reasons for pursuing a doctoral degree—their jobs and careers depend on it. Others have driving personal reasons, such as adding to their power, authority, and sense of confidence. Others made promises to themselves and others that they are determined not to break. And some, I discovered, simply love to study and are driven by a curiosity to learn how to do research. The doctoral program provides the structure and social support that allow them to do this. But they also had another quality that would get them through, and it was not brilliance. It was tenacity and a long-term, evolving vision of completing this intellectual journey.

Nevertheless, if students are not sure why they are in the doctoral program or want a degree, or if they are ambivalent about their decision to study or about the career it might lead to, or if they have no long-term vision for themselves, or if reasons in general are weak, then trouble lies ahead. There are many weak reasons. Here are just a few: You are ambivalent about your decision to study in this particular program, but you are not sure what else to study; you want to stay with or join your friends who got in the program; you enjoyed your master's-level work and would like to continue this kind of studying; you are not sure what else to do in your life right now; the degree might be useful later; your government will pay so why not take advantage of this opportunity; you'd like to see "PhD" or "EdD" after your name on your business card. In these cases, the inner drive needed to devote many years to sometimes grueling work might not be there. In other words, there needs to be a long-term reason for and commitment to *getting* the degree, not just having it.

⌒ Common Reasons for Dropping Out

Many students drop out of doctoral programs, at least in the United States (Golde, 2005, says up to 40 percent), perhaps with good reason, but also because they might not have been prepared for what they were getting themselves into. Lovitts (2001, p. 1) called the high attrition rate an "invisible problem." Once students disappear, schools do not usually follow up to ascertain why. My guess is that your own university does not advertise that 30%–50% of its doctoral students never finish, or that it probably has not taken serious steps to investigate reasons for high attrition.

As Golde (2005) pointed out in her interview study of 58 doctoral students from four departments who left their programs, students need to be well integrated into both the discipline and their departments. If they are not, the lack of fit is often the result of student isolation or a mismatch (p. 671). Lovitts (2001) concluded that the problem lies mainly with the structure and culture of graduate departments. Her study was instrumental in helping Golde frame her own findings as "lack of fit." However, lack of fit might not be obvious from early stages in the program. Golde's (2000) own case studies of three students who dropped out showed that they were all content in the first year or two of doctoral study. Problems developed later, particularly with advisers (see Chapter 7) and lack of departmental support. One student simply lost interest in studying because he became involved in lucrative work as a computer specialist in Silicon Valley. In any case, Golde (2005, p. 696) concluded by asserting that "early attrition is preferable to late attrition" (a great saving of stress and finances) but that "nonetheless, the interviews show that a good deal of attrition is unnecessary and preventable."

Here is a story of attrition, paraphrased from Golde (2000), one of the three in-depth case studies in this article.

Story: Jane's decision to drop out of her doctoral program

> Jane was interested in art history and had worked at a museum for four years. She spent some time in Italy, and a friend there persuaded her to apply to a doctoral program in the United States. She got accepted, had a wonderful year and a half in the program, and got along well with faculty and fellow students. She liked her classes and learned how think analytically and theoretically, skills she was grateful for acquiring. She initially got along very well with her adviser and got all As in classes with him. But something happened at the proposal stage. First, Jane's adviser assigned her a dissertation topic, rather than letting Jane construct her own topic. Second, he refused to accept the gender-oriented take she wished to explore. From that point, the adviser let Jane know that he didn't think she was capable of writing a dissertation. At about the same time, she had a serious car accident. In a state of shock and depression, she ended up seeking counseling at a school clinic, regrouping, and starting work on a new topic with a new adviser. But before finishing her proposal in her second year, she suddenly decided to quit the program.
>
> In the interview with Golde later, Jane realized that there had been problems from the beginning. She said to Golde: "In all honesty I had some ambivalence about the PhD before I came here, but I thought, 'Well, I am just going to do the degree and be a professor.'" (p. 214). She did not pay sufficient attention at the beginning to her ambivalent feelings about doing a doctoral degree in art history and wished she had done the soul-searching work much earlier. Then came the

car accident, the shocking dismissal by her first adviser, her shifting interest and realization she did not really want to be a professor of art history, her loss of confidence in academia, her growing sense of isolation, the lack of strong departmental support, and her sense that faculty were really more interested in their own work than in her.

Jane summed up her reflections on what the problems were this way: " 'I think the advisor is 80% of the deal. If you get along really well, and that person is there to support you and you exchange ideas well, I think it can be the driving force. . . . And I think that you have to have a love of being on your own and just digging. I am really a people-oriented person, and I start talking to the books, and they weren't talking back. It seems like something you should know, but I just didn't realize how intensely isolated it is.' " (Golde, 2000, p. 217)

I am particularly moved by Jane's comment that she found herself talking to her books, and they weren't talking back. Among many other things that Jane, as a social and people-oriented person, was not prepared for, was a major one: the isolation of doctoral research, particularly when a committed and encouraging adviser was lacking. But she started the program with ambivalent feelings about becoming an art history professor—feelings she did not acknowledge until it was too late.

Knowing the Demands, Procedures, and Resources at Your University

It pays to know something about the demands, procedures, and resources at a university before you start, or are too far along in, a doctoral program. The students I worked with in Japan had little choice as to where to pursue an American university doctoral degree: There was only one place in Japan to do this. Learning about the demands, procedures, and resources of the university came after they decided to begin their doctoral program rather than before. But this information not only can assist students in making decisions about where to study but can also prepare them for what is to come. Everyone should do this homework, early on. Web sources, departmental literature, currently enrolled students, recent graduates, and professors and administrators are all sources of useful information.

Here are some basic questions about demands and procedures:

- What information can you find in the university's Graduate Student Handbook or program handbook? (How carefully have you read this material and how often do you return to it?)

- How are students selected for admission?

- If students apply to a school in order to work with a particular faculty member, is this person instrumental in getting them accepted?

- What are the topics of inquiry and publication records of faculty that students might want to work with?

- Is there financial aid at this school? If so, for how long, and what must students do to get it and keep it?

- How many credits are required to graduate?

- How much course work is there?

- What are the required and elective courses?

- Must students be enrolled full time at any point?

- Must they be continuously enrolled (no gaps)?

- Who is responsible for selecting or changing their advisers?

- What procedures are needed to advance to doctoral candidacy, such a oral exams or papers?

- What kind of dissertation proposal is required, and is there an oral defense at the proposal stage?

- Is there a time limit for completing the dissertation?

- What happens if students cannot finish by the deadline?

- What must their dissertation consist of and what must it look like?

- What will the dissertation defense consist of, and who is responsible for selecting people to be on a defense committee?

- At any stage of the doctoral program journey, are there forms that need to be filled out and submitted to the proper committees or people (e.g., IRB forms; see Chapter 4).

- And, even if it might be difficult to uncover this information, what are the graduation and attrition rates in the department?

Equally important for students to know are the human and material resources available in their programs and the reputations of programs and faculty advisers for supporting (financially, psychologically) students over a period of years. As previous research has shown, departmental and faculty support are essential for helping students integrate into the doctoral program. Lack of support, or lack of fit, can lead to high attrition rates, as described by Golde (2005), Lovitts (2001), and others. Having a good adviser or supervisor who can also play the role of mentor has been found to be central to students' success and satisfaction (Belcher, 1994; Creighton, Creighton, & Parks, 2010; Ives & Rowley, 2005; Lunsford, 2012; Simpson & Matsuda, 2008; Thein & Beach, 2010). Sometimes students are fortunate enough to come across such a person by chance; usually, locating the right person takes active searching and negotiating on the part of students inside and even outside their departments. However, both in the United States and in the U.K. system, there seems to be a variety of adviser-supervisor styles, not all of which are equally helpful for students (Delamont, Parry, & Atkinson, 1998; see more on advisers, supervisors, and mentors in Chapter 7). Among other strategies, students can learn by word of mouth from other students early in their program about which professors to seek out and which ones to avoid.

Other resources are important to know about as well. What kind of library does the university have, and how extensive are its holdings in areas that students are interested in? What kinds of electronic data bases and resources are accessible to students and is there a computer support lab? Is there a good student mailing list system whereby all students in a cohort or program can receive news and updates? Are there any student-run conferences or publications in the department that can provide opportunities for students to test out ideas and research plans? What staff are available, other than professors, to answer questions and provide guidance and counseling (e.g., in offices, libraries, counseling centers)?

The point is: Know ahead of time, or as early as possible, what the demands, procedures, and resources are at the university(-ies) you are interested in or already enrolled in.

☞ L2 Issues

If English is not your first language, you might be overwhelmed at the quantity of difficult reading and writing that you need to do in a doctoral program. However, if you got through a master's program in the medium of English, have succeeded in previous academic reading and writing activities in English, have been accepted to an English-medium doctoral program by means of samples of your own writing, and have already begun to do passing work in your doctoral courses, then your non-native English proficiency will be a minor hindrance. Many dissertation writers, both L1 and L2, enlist the help of copyeditors or proofreaders as they prepare their final drafts, so I suggest not worrying about problems with English, particularly at these early stages. Do your best, and then ask for help. In fact, everyone in a doctoral program faces similar hurdles: Academic discourse is a "second" language to everyone, full of terminology (necessary), jargon (needless and pretentious), formal turns of phrases, and unfamiliar research methods, theories, and philosophical stances (Casanave, 2008). The volume of reading and writing required in a doctoral program is overwhelming for everyone, and everyone is obligated to seek short cuts, editorial help, and strategies for dovetailing. Your ability to think, learn, and improve is as good as the next person's. (*Note:* Some of the best writers I have known are L2 users of English; some of the worst are native English speakers. Being a native speaker of English does not automatically mean a person is a good writer or efficient reader.)

That said, if you are a multilingual-multicultural-translingual person (whatever label you wish to apply), your L1(s) can work greatly to your advantage if you plan to do a dissertation project that includes people and places from your own background. You will have insider access to people, documents, cultural knowledge, and multilingual resources that your monolingual English-speaking classmates do not. You will also eventually be able to share your research findings in publications in local languages unavailable to researchers who are not bilingual (Lillis & Curry, 2010; Curry & Lillis, 2013). So do not despair and do not complain. Use your linguistic and cultural resources to your advantage and get help as needed. Everyone does. Your L2 status is an asset, and know that all English users, L1 and L2 alike, benefit from continuing to polish their language skills throughout life. Nevertheless, it is also the case that in most multilingual-multicultural research, the issue of translation will arise, both in data collection and in data representation. Whether you are collecting data and writing in your L1 or L2, it is a good idea to have another knowledgeable bilingual to check and assist with translations.

☞ Quality-of-Life Issues

In my original plan for this book, I had placed a chapter at the end on quality-of-life issues. A nice send-off to readers, I thought. But a perceptive reviewer suggested I move this discussion earlier, as something that needs to be considered from the beginning of doctoral study, so that by dissertation time, healthy and balanced life habits have become routine. Sometimes doctoral students think about quality-of-life issues when it is too late to help them through the last stages of their dissertation projects. I have worked with students at this stage who suffer from eye strain; shoulder, back, and neck problems; strained relationships with family and friends; poor diets; lack of sleep; lack of exercise; and a general lack of fun in their lives. Don't be one of those students. Even those with chronic health problems can find a way to let the doctoral program improve the quality of their lives (Okada, 2008).

Health

I have heard myself say to students many times during the course of doctoral work, especially as the dissertation project looms, that their health needs to take top priority. I will not dwell on this because it is such commonsense advice as to be incontestable: If you are not healthy, you can't do anything else that you need to do. I am sure that all of us have tried to do some academic writing or reading while we have a cold or flu or after several nights of insufficient sleep, only to find that our brains are dead and we have wasted time sitting in front of our computers. Our time would be better spent drinking some hot chicken broth or fresh ginger tea and sleeping for a day or two. Once we recover, we can work twice as quickly and easily make up for lost time. If you are struck down with something more serious, take care of this first—take a leave of absence if necessary, but don't ignore it and don't give up your long-term goal. If you find yourself never exercising or moving from your hunched over position at the computer, and then waking up one day wracked with back and shoulder and neck pain, your distress could have been predicted. It is better to exercise in some form or another every day; use this time not only to loosen up stiff joints and muscles but also to do some quality thinking, to solve writing and reading problems, and to plan new ideas. I am known around my hometown as the woman who reads and speed walks at the same time, so I kill two birds with one stone. I accomplish in an hour what would take me two hours if I were to do these activities separately. (And no, I have not yet fallen down or stepped in dog poop.)

Fatigue

Connected to good health is good sleep, both in quality and quantity. This is another issue that needs little discussion because it is so commonsensical. You can do the experiment on yourself: Compare what you can accomplish academically when you are refreshed and when you are sleep-deprived. When you are refreshed, you are likely to accomplish twice as much in half the time. And though it might be hard advice for some people to follow, if you have sleep problems, do not work late into the night. If you do, you might find that you have to medicate yourself to get to sleep, a strategy to be avoided if at all possible.

Isolation

The doctoral program is really two programs rolled into one, as Sternberg (1981) reminded us a long time ago: the course work stage and the dissertation stage. The course work stage is vibrant, full of people and social and intellectual stimulation, good discussion of shared readings, study sessions, and even partying. However, when course work is over, classmates often scatter, especially if they do not live on or near campus or have student offices on campus. Even if they do, isolation is endemic at the dissertation stage. Students are isolated from each other, buried in their own high-pressure intellectual worlds. Study groups at the dissertation stage are rare, partly because it becomes increasingly hard for classmates to focus on each other's work as their own projects take off in individual directions. Where can they find the time to focus on their classmates' projects as well as on their own? They tend to be isolated from families as well—locked away in their rooms or offices, immersed in esoteric ideas and language that their families can no longer understand. Moreover, after course work, professors are no longer a steady presence in students' lives, and advisers and supervisors might wish to see their advisees only occasionally, and only when the students have a piece of writing ready to receive feedback on.

Isolation can be deadly. Do what you can to avoid it. Even one or two steady friends and classmates to consult with regularly can save you from succumbing to this deadly disease. Think ahead to how you might prevent isolation at the dissertation stage—find any way you can to stay connected to your department and to some of your classmates. (See Kuwahara, 2008, on this topic, and a story from her in Chapter 8; see also Van Cleave and Bridges-Rhoads, 2013.)

Real-Life Demands (Work, Family, Relationships)

I have been so astonished at how some of my doctoral students in Japan manage their real-life demands during the course of their doctoral study that I wrote about this a few years ago (Casanave, 2010a). Somehow these students (most mid-career, middle-aged) juggle full-time jobs or a series of part-time jobs, a family life of some kind that might include care of children or elderly parents or in-laws, relationships with partners or spouses or close friends, and doctoral study (evening and weekend classes, followed by dissertation work whenever possible). At the dissertation writing stage, this juggling act becomes a five-ring circus, ready to spin out of control at any moment. Maybe this is a common problem at the dissertation stage. By this time, money and time are running out, and students need to get back to work and to their home towns or countries. How does it ever all get done? I have one student, an American man who works at his university sometimes six days a week, who has confessed that he has to wait till vacations to get any work done on his dissertation. I also recall one of my own advisers, Arthur Applebee, telling his students that if we wait to work on dissertations only during vacations, we will never finish. Data get cold. We run out of steam. Life takes over. Work and family obligations take precedence. And suddenly we find we have run out of time.

There are no easy solutions to this problem. I recall classmates in my own doctoral program whose relationships were strained, whose marriages ended in divorce, and whose friendships ended when one could no longer focus sufficiently on the life and work of the other. Most people cannot quit their jobs, although I have several students who were able to take sabbatical leaves at crucial dissertation points. I know a couple of others who took voluntary unpaid leave from their teaching positions or even quit their jobs in order to finish. But if you are prepared for possible strains ahead of time, you can plan ahead:

- Help friends and family and partners understand what you are going through and why. Do this regularly.

- Seek counseling (on campus, if available) if the strains are causing unbearable misery.

- Nourish your bonds and close connections with a handful of people you don't want to lose.

- Above all, keep a vision of the post-dissertation future ahead of you.

Juggling Priorities and Managing Time

By putting together issues from the preceding sections, you can see how important it is to find ways to juggle priorities, balance life activities and relationships, and manage time (cf. Paltridge & Woodrow, 2012). Part of managing time well is realizing that no matter what you do, it is not possible to get everything done that you want to get done. It just won't happen. Hence the priorities: Health first, lifelong important relationships second, and then some kind of balance between work obligations and the dissertation project.

Summary of Main Points in This Chapter

1. There are strong and weak reasons for deciding to pursue a doctoral degree. A long-term vision and commitment are essential.

2. Doctoral student attrition is high, caused by many factors, including students' lack of clear goals, absence of strong interest and support by advisers and departments, and changes of goals.

3. Every university has demands and procedures to be followed for the doctoral degree that need to be understood by each student in a program.

4. If English is not your first language, there are ways to make your bilingual status work for you, even though multilingual research is complex. Translation of data to English is a challenge. L1 users of English who are collecting data from L2 participants face issues of translation too. Plan ahead.

5. Quality-of-life issues need to be addressed early in a doctoral program so that routines of good health and relationships are established from the beginning, before damage to both occurs later in the program.

☞ *Suggestions for Discussion and Reflection* ☜

1. If you have not reflected deeply on this question yet in written or spoken conversations with yourself and trusted friends, do so now: Why do you want or need a doctoral degree? How strong do you believe your desire is? What factors might cause you to shift your goals? What might the consequence be for you of pushing ahead? Of dropping out?

2. What demands and procedures exist at your own university for completing the various stages of the doctoral program? If you are not sure, where can you find this information? What support resources are there to help students in your department through the program?

3. If you think you might construct a dissertation project where more than one language is involved, what issues do you see arising for you?

4. Discuss or write about the quality-of-life issues mentioned in this chapter, and comment on how relevant they are to your own situation. What other factors might influence the quality of your life during doctoral study? What strategies can you use to maintain health and balance in your life during the stressful doctoral years?

5. Try to find out what students from your program do after graduating with their doctoral degree.

Chapter 3

Writing Research Memos and Dissertation Journals

In the Introduction to *Before the Dissertation*, I stated firmly that this is not a book about how to write a doctoral dissertation. You know by now that it is not. However, the main message of this important chapter is that there are numerous other kinds of essential writing besides the dissertation itself. All of these essential kinds of writing begin before you even start to write your proposal and continue throughout the research and writing process. This is not good news for people who dislike writing or who agonize over writing of any kind. But writing is what doctoral students do. All the time.

The good news is that the kinds of writing I describe in this chapter will all contribute to your dissertation in some way. They might help clarify or focus your thinking, help you work through confusions and frustrations, turn into bits of writing that might actually end up in your proposal or dissertation, be a repository of records and decisions, and serve as an emotional outlet. Moreover, they are not required by your professors, they are not graded or evaluated by anyone, and they are unconstrained in style, format, and approach. It is writing that is (to a greater or lesser degree) personal, reflective, technical (e.g., a kind of record keeping), and creative. No one but yourself will tell you how much to write, how often to write, what writing tools to use (paper, pencil, computer, even audio-recorder), or what to write, and no one will correct or care about your grammar and spelling. It is writing that serves your purposes only, and will thus be done differently by every doctoral student. You can also label these kinds of writing any way you want (see the full description of different kinds of research journals in Casanave, 2011).

I wish I could say that all of my own doctoral students have followed my suggestions (urgings, pleadings, beggings) to regularly engage in some kind of reflective writing, but only some have done so. I have seen the benefits in all cases where they have. Here is one extended commentary, used with permission, from a former student, who sent this email about her own journals and memos after reading an earlier draft of this chapter. Her abbreviations are kept as she wrote them:

> Following your advice, I kept everything related to my
> diss[ertation] (with the exception of reflections and journals
> which I kept in a computer file) in a single notebook. This
> was one of the most useful and practical advice I got from

you in your Narrative and Case study course. (I vividly recall how I wished I got this advice from day one of my doctoral studies!) If I wrote something on a post-it or a small piece of paper, I would paste it on. Until then, I often lost bits of memos and such because they were scattered in different places. I brought the notebook when I had meetings w/ you and D. (my advisors) and others such as people like Y. Everything was in there; including brief reflections, questions I had, names of authors and book titles, and other notes to assist my cognition. Some parts weren't used in the diss, but I found them useful later on. It was also useful to trace back my own trajectory, because it showed how my thoughts and diss project as a whole came together and also evolved. I still have these two small notebooks. They are rather dirty because I carried them around, but to this day, they are valuable sources of info. (Hanako Okada email communication, August 21, 2013)

I am not alone in calling for some kind of reflective writing during doctoral study. Maxwell (2005, 2012) advocated, and gave examples of, "research memos" in which students worked out ideas and made plans or, in the form of "research identity memos," made explicit their own assumptions and subjectivities in a project. Another kind of informal writing, field notes, is essential in certain kinds of qualitative research that involve naturalistic observations (Wolcott, 2001, pp. 99–100). Field notes may be used in all kinds of research and take numerous forms that include both record keeping and reflection in a field note journal (Sunstein & Chiseri-Strater, 2002, Chapter 2). Silverman and Marvasti (2008, drawing from Cryer, 1996) comment on the importance of "research diaries" (pp. 301–304) in their chapter called Keeping a Record. In master's and doctoral courses I have taught, I asked all students to write reading-response journals (ungraded), hoping to help them develop a habit of continuing to write later in response to the readings they would do for their dissertations.

In the case of my own dissertation work, I wrote three kinds of journals (described in Casanave, 2011): field note journals, dissertation journals, and "academic letters" to my adviser. I made notes of all of my observations of classes that were part of the data collection in my research setting in my field note journals, which were handwritten, dated, and page-numbered. My ongoing decisions, dilemmas, questions, descriptions, responses to readings, evolving interpretations, and personal and emotional states were recorded in my dissertation journals. These were hardbound journal books, pages already numbered, that were designed to be used by law students for case work. I wrote both of these journals by hand and filled six books over several years. In recent years, I shifted to word processing for some of this kind of writing but am more attached emotionally to the physical journals. Less private were the writings I shared early in my planning stages with my adviser. I wrote her what I called "academic letters" (cf. Danielewicz, 1999) instead of early drafts of "real" writing, which I was not yet ready to do. These academic letters were word-processed, started out as real letters, but quickly morphed into discussions of my readings and ideas I was pondering, and ended with a formal reference list of all the work I had cited in the letter. I couldn't seem to make myself just start out with a literature-review type of writing, but I could write my way into this kind of writing by beginning with a letter. Some of the bits and pieces of these very long letters I later pasted into dissertation drafts. My adviser kindly penciled in some comments and questions and returned the letters to me, which I still have saved in a large envelope. (See examples from an academic letter that doubled as a course paper and from my dissertation journals at the end of this chapter.)

I can imagine many other kinds of formats for this essential "non-essential" writing, done by hand or by computer. Sketches and brainstorm-bubble maps and flow charts, done by hand or computer, might be suitable for doodlers. Coffee-shop addicts will collect notes they have made on paper napkins. Diary-keepers will write secretly and personally, transforming feelings and ideas into words for no one else to see. Some people will talk into an audio-recorder that they carry with them everywhere. I know one person who sometimes writes himself reminders and brief thoughts with ballpoint pen on the palm of his hand. The formats do not matter. But the ongoing transformation of ideas and observations into words and images does.

In the remainder of this chapter, I describe some of the important things to write about in the early stages of doctoral dissertation work, each of which can assist dissertation writers later: writing about readings, ideas and experiences, decisions and emotions.

☞ Writing about Readings

Every scholar, from novice to established, needs a system for recording bibliographic information, for writing summaries of and commentaries on readings, and for keeping track of key quotes (with page numbers) for possible use later. I wonder if people do these by hand anymore (see Carnell, et al., 2008, for evidence that some senior scholars still do), or if computer files are now ubiquitous. It is certainly easy to sort things and find things if one has reading notes in a computer file, unless, like me, one's files are scattered in many different folders according to project (now where did I put my reading notes on X???). Still, some people might like the comfort of an actual notebook, the slide of a favorite pencil or pen over paper, and the way a simple notebook will not let the writer become distracted with emails, web searches, or the dozens of other possibilities for interruption when one is staring at the computer screen. Just now, sitting here in the school library and looking out the big picture window on the second floor as the wind started to get quite fierce, I stopped tapping on my lap top keys to check the Monterey weather on the Internet. I can't seem to help myself.

Decades ago a professor I admired in my own doctoral program showed me his very low-tech method of writing or typing all needed information about each reading on individual 5x7 index cards—these could then be sorted differently for each project he was working on. He recorded full bibliographic information at the top of the card, followed by a few lines of commentary to remind him of what the reading was about and his reaction to it, and then relevant quotes, with page numbers. I used this system for many years, and my stack of index cards is still on my shelf, about six inches high. I liked watching it grow over time and pulling out and resorting cards I needed for individual projects. But, with mixed feelings, I now write all my notes into computer files. Whatever system we use, a reading-response resource (journal, cards, computer file) needs full bibliographic information, a brief comment to remind us what the content of the reading is, selected quotes with page numbers that we think might be useful later, and some kind of commentary from the heart or head (emotional, quizzical, or critical). Readers who are inspired or enraged or puzzled might write extensive commentary—always fun to reread later, particularly if the commentary connects with your own life or if someday you get to meet the author in person.

Here is one word of caution about reading response journals: **If text is copied exactly from a reading into a handwritten journal or computer file, without quote marks and page numbers, it becomes easy later to (inadvertently) cut and paste such pieces into a dissertation draft, without the writer's recalling whether the extract was an exact quote, a paraphrase, or her own commentary.** Even if the extract turns into a true paraphrase, page numbers might be needed if the ideas are particular to the author of the book or article. The danger of plagiarism arises in such cases, an academic mistake (I cannot use the word *crime*) that can have dire consequences for writers (Abasi, Akbari, & Graves, 2008; Eisner & Vicinus, 2008; Gu & Brooks, 2008; Howard, 1995; Li & Casanave, 2012). In other words, the purpose of a reading journal is not just to record ideas and quotes, but to keep track of the precise source of all information for use later.

Finally, a system of keeping track of readings, quotes, and commentary is essential long before it comes time to write a literature review (more on this later). Depending on the kind of dissertation you do, you may draw on hundreds of sources. When it is time to write a proposal and dissertation, it is too late to start searching for, reading, and organizing these hundreds of readings. This time-consuming work has to be started early. If you are not good at devising a system on your own, then look into data management software especially designed for academia, such as Endnote (http://endnote.com) or Mendely (http://www.mendeley.com). (For a comparison of many reference management systems, see the Wikipedia site: http://en.wikipedia.org/wiki/Comparison_of_reference_management_software.)

☞ Writing about Ideas and Experiences

If it looks like your dissertation project will grow out of your own ideas and experiences, as many dissertations do, you need to start writing about these from the earliest stages of dissertation planning. Some of these research memos or personal journal entries might simply seem self-indulgent or excessively autobiographical, but I disagree. They can form the heart of your rationale for a project, helping you figure out why you are interested in exploring certain topics and making the needed links between the personal and research aspects of a project. This kind of rationale might even be a required part of the introduction to the dissertation itself. Writing early on about ideas and experiences in the form of journals or memos can also immerse you in the writing and thinking that you would need to do anyway, guide you into the nooks and crannies of a project, and help you begin making links between you and your participants, research settings, and research issues. Here is a story about one of my doctoral students, who wrote research memos as a technique for working her way into her dissertation proposal.

Story: Laura and her research memos

>One of my doctoral students, a mid-career Japanese-American woman with a family and tenured job in Japan, wanted to write her dissertation proposal before she took a year-long sabbatical in her childhood home of Seattle. She had lost a year to illness, her confidence and energy were low, and she knew only that she had an ongoing interest in the experiences of herself and other Japanese-American university teachers in Japan. A number of these friends and colleagues met over the years, and sometimes presented panels at local conferences on what it meant to be American but look Japanese, to raise children in the Japanese education system, to face skeptical Japanese students and colleagues who were expecting that native English–speaking teachers were all white, and to deal with their own lack of full proficiency in Japanese. I was in California at the time, but we talked by skype and wrote back and forth about this for a long time before Laura left Japan for her sabbatical. At the time she was not sure how these personal, deep-seated, and emotional interests could turn into real research. I was completely convinced this could turn into a fascinating dissertation topic and was also certain she could get a proposal written and defended before she left on sabbatical.

The challenge to actually draft a proposal can be scary and cause writer's block and loss of confidence. So I asked her to write research memos and journal entries, both on her readings at this stage and, importantly, on what was motivating her interest in the experiences of Japanese-Americans in Japan. In the months before she finally finished the draft of her proposal, she wrote six major journal entries about herself and her current thinking about her own experiences in Japan and how some of her readings were enlightening her understanding. Each entry had a title that expressed the theme of that entry, a technique she continued to use when she wrote research memos at the dissertation writing stage, when she was beginning to analyze the experiences of her case study participants. I responded to all of the entries with comments and questions. Over the months, Laura put together a wonderful proposal, passed her proposal defense just before leaving for Seattle, and collected as many interviews with other Japanese Americans as she could.

In Seattle, she was faced with the task of beginning to write something for the dissertation itself. But from what I could see, this writing seemed to come much more naturally thanks to her previous regular memo writing. Her early writing consisted of stories about her participants, links she made to readings, ties with her own experiences. She didn't call her initial writing "chapters." They were just more formal journal entries, bits of writing, as it were, but this time mainly about the experiences of her participants. In writing about her participants, she was also writing about herself, and continued to do this as an insider participant in her own research project. It all worked. Much of this writing found its way into her dissertation drafts.

In November, 2013, Laura successfully defended her full dissertation, which three committee members described as "beautifully written."

In short, this kind of writing about self, one's own ideas, and one's own experiences can be quite liberating. It can unblock writers by giving them permission to write about themselves and to find their way into their projects without fear of evaluation or embarrassment. But students who want to share personal experiences with an adviser or faculty respondent need to trust their reader completely—to trust that no personal stories will prejudice the readers' estimation of the student in any way nor ever be used against her to impede her progress. If students do not have such a trusted faculty adviser, then I urge them to seek a collegial writing partner from among classmates or friends for their most personal writing, and to write more cautiously to their advisers. Even writing in a personal journal that is not read by anyone is better than not writing anything. The point is to write.

ᔐ Writing about Decisions

My own dissertation journals were a mix of writings, including reflections on my evolving ideas, on participants I had found, on readings, and on relations with my adviser(s). But also they were the place where I recorded decisions that I made as I went along, and the confusions and frustrations I felt in getting to the point where I could make decisions (see the next section, Writing about Emotions). One of the hardest decisions I had to make was to let a participant go who was not working out. Up to that point, I had considered him to be a central figure in my study and I wrote about him a lot in my journal (see the example at the end of this chapter). New to research like this and to the difficult process of interviewing participants from cultures and language backgrounds other than mine, I wondered if there was anything I could have done to prevent this loss of a participant. Perhaps a more experienced researcher would have recognized earlier that the participant had to be let go. But in my dissertation journals, I made and recorded this decision late, after much frustration and self-blame. The journal records how I tried to figure out what was going wrong, who I talked to about my lack of success with this participant, and the final outcome. This was just one decision of many that I recorded in these journals.

All early dissertation planners and writers can benefit from a record of decisions of some kind, with entries recorded by date and page number. You can use the information to write about the dissertation process later, as needed for a methods chapter or an interim report to an adviser. You can also use it help you later reflect on methods and decisions—a necessary part of the conclusions to most dissertations. Of course, decisions do not need to be recorded in journal entry form (this was my choice)—they could just as easily be recorded in a spreadsheet or list or table of some kind. The point is to make some kind of record of decisions along the way.

⌒ Writing about Emotions

Probably the most personal kind of reflective writing during the dissertation journey is the truly personal journal-style genre, unseen by anyone but the writer. It is here that struggling doctoral students can rant, explode, weep, despair, exalt, celebrate, laugh, and agonize. Emotions like these should not be taken lightly and certainly not dismissed as unimportant or as signs of weakness. They are normal, even for established academics. I know that women are stereotypically said to be better at expressing emotions than are men, but some of the most emotional people I know are men, even if they pretend to hide their feelings. Emotions are physical, says Damasio (1994, 1999): neurological, chemical responses to events and thoughts in our lives, and thus not to be denied or devalued.

Writing about the negative emotions can defuse them and put them into perspective. Toxins are released, anger expressed without verbal or physical violence to others. Negative emotions in a doctoral program are not inevitable, but common for those students who last past the first couple of years. One of many reasons is that doctoral departments can be hotbeds of neglect, abuse, humiliation, competition, frustration, and scandal, in addition to engendering the normal emotions that students feel as they try to get a dissertation completed (Sternberg's [1981] stories about neglectful and abusive doctoral advisers are a bit daunting in this regard). Writing about the positive emotions is equally important. Written documentation of positive emotions can provide concrete evidence that things are not as bleak as they sometimes seem. It can allow students to celebrate important successes, whether large or small, in writing. A record of success is just as important as is an outlet for pain. The painful moments do stand out and tend to be the subject of complaint, counseling, and nasty gossip, but the positive moments are the survival mechanisms.

☞ Concluding Cautions

Keep all of your personal, reflective, and decision-making writing in a safe place. This includes substantive email, if you do much of your thinking-writing by email to a friend. Send a dated copy to yourself, or copy your email into a word file each time you write, and make some kind of back-up in whatever system you feel is safe and reliable.

⌒ Two Sample Writings

1. From an academic letter to my adviser that also served as a course paper:

June 14, 1986

Dear Judith,

My paper to you this quarter will be a letter. A letter seems to be the only format that is appropriate for my stage of thinking. I will double space it, however, and list all references as needed as a separate item. In this letter I hope to address the following issues: (1) my present worries, doubts and confusions; (2) the population and setting I continue to be interested in; (3) the relation between our course on oral and written language and the population and setting I'm interested in; (4) where I might go next as I move towards a proposal.

I am experiencing the same frustrations that many of my colleagues have gone/are going through in the pre-proposal and proposal stage. One of the fears that pervades my thinking is that of triviality. On some days everything I read and think seems trivial. On other days only my own thinking seems trivial. And on a few days, when the sun is shining and the cat is purring, not even my own thinking seems trivial.

My big worry. Many issues in educational research appear to emerge from intuitive common sense notions about what is already clearly and obviously known and happening in classrooms, in language development, in pedagogy. I am often struck with the question: Why study this? Everyone knows this. Why do we need research to prove it (which it never can do anyway; it can only "suggest"—a word that gets on my nerves when I'm in my trivial moods). [... 22 more double-spaced pages, plus three-page reference list]

2. From an early dissertation journal in which I recorded details of my first interactions with participants. This entry is about a Chinese man, CL, who struck everyone, even the other Chinese doctoral students, as very eccentric and difficult. I should have let him go as a participant much earlier than I did.

October 25, 1987

During class break Thursday [I was observing a first year sociology doctoral core course] I went to CL to get the papers he was supposed to bring and to make an appointment for the next post-[written]exercise interview. He didn't have them and didn't want to meet next week after class, even tho' he agreed the previous day that that was a better time. I just don't know how to get past his layers of defenses. I don't know how much of his uncooperative behavior is normal for him in China. [. . .]

We had a post exercise 2 interview Wednesday morning. He came too late to do it, and didn't have his papers. He tried to convince me to talk to him by phone in the evening [. . .] He tried to convince me his exercises are not interesting, that he is not taking them seriously. Somehow I doubt that this means he will be more willing to work with me on his papers. I wonder who he thinks I am. To what extent are culture shock, fear, panic, and discomfort playing a part in all this? What does he really think of this sociology class and this department? [. . .]

[Many months later, I recorded that I lost my temper with CL, something a researcher should never do, and let him go as a participant. Eight months after the October 25 entry, I ran into to him, and he told me he had decided to leave the sociology department and "go to Yale to study art."] Dissertation Journal Book 2, May 19, 1988

Summary of Main Points in This Chapter

1. Numerous kinds of personal and reflective writing, sometimes considered unimportant or a waste of time, are in fact crucial for getting unformed ideas, intuitions, and experiences into words at early stages of a dissertation project.

2. Dissertation journals, research memos and diaries, field note journals, academic letters, and other inventive kinds of writing are done for the writer alone, even if shared with an adviser or colleague, and hence are unconstrained by rules and conventions.

3. Among other possibilities, several kinds of personal writing stand out: Writing about readings, about ideas and experiences, about decisions, and about emotions.

4. Some pieces of this kind of writing might find their way into the proposal or dissertation itself.

5. It is important to have a system, however personal, for keeping track of what you read, think, decide, and feel during the dissertation journey.

☞ *Suggestions for Discussion and Reflection* ☜

1. What kinds of personal and reflective writing, if any, have you done in your academic life so far? What were their purposes and how well were those purposes served?

2. What system(s) do you have for keeping track of what you read? What changes, if any, would you like to make to this system?

3. What outlets for the emotions that are part of normal graduate work do you have? Do any of these outlets involve writing?

Chapter 4

Initial Thoughts on Topics

Let me begin with the confession that I do not know to what extent topic development in the preparation of doctoral dissertations is a problem. My experience that it is difficult might be unique or it might be more typical than many of us would like to admit. I also don't know if students who wish to pursue qualitative topics have more problems than those who pursue more conventional quantitative or mixed method topics (I suspect they do—qualitative projects can be very messy). I don't know how many students start over (as I and a couple of my doctoral classmates did) if their initial ideas don't work out. I don't know how many advisers monitor students' topic development from early or late stages or how such guidance takes place. And I don't know whether many doctoral programs offer early courses that focus on topic development. (Courses in proposal writing often come too late, or at inappropriate times, given that people write proposals after they have found topics they wish to explore, even if the specifics are not clear at the proposal stage. Courses in statistics, taken early, convey the myth that with some topics, objectivity and truth of some kind are possible.) These are all questions for doctoral students to think about and to talk to others about, early in the doctoral program.

In spite of what I don't know about the topic-development problem, I have found it odd that the literature on feedback and on doctoral dissertation writing (articles, guidebooks) does not talk more about topic construction, which I have found to be one of the most difficult aspects of doctoral student research. I use the term *construction* intentionally, not topic *choice,* to indicate that a topic for an individual project is built, creatively constructed, over time, from a complex array of internal and external forces and factors. The word *choice* implies that topics are already out there, waiting to be selected. I suppose this might happen if an adviser provides students with a list of topics to choose from or if a student is part of a tightly run group research project in which the adviser doles out pieces to all his followers. But in my experience, topic construction is more common than topic choice, particularly for a "topic that works."

By a "topic that works" I mean a topic (a) that stems from some strong drive, curiosity, or passion within the individual— from something connected to her life and her interests, including the type of job she might seek in the future; (b) that is suitable for research at the dissertation level at a particular institution, within a particular (sub)field, and in conjunction with at least one compatible adviser; and (c) that has long-term staying power, such that it will hold the student's interest and maintain her energy over some years, and possibly into a post-PhD career. These points are often made in some of the literature on dissertation writing, but not dwelt upon. Moreover, a "topic that works" is not one in which the student researcher starts out seeking fixed answers, truth, or objective proof. Such a search is fruitless, at least in the social sciences, so it is not a good place to begin. Begin with questions, and hope to end with more and better questions.

☞ Some Common Problems with Topic Development

Initial plans for topics often don't work. Here are two scenarios we can imagine, among many. First, it can come as a great shock to suddenly have to come up with a realistic and do-able dissertation topic at the proposal stage if students do not have topic construction in mind from fairly early in course work. Playing with different ideas during course work allows students to test out various ideas and make changes and adjustments without feeling rushed or trapped. It is not possible to develop a topic for a major research project overnight, despite what some of the guides say ("brainstorm a list of possible topics; choose one"). Moreover, I think it is quite common for students to have a least one false start, requiring them to start over. I include myself and some of my former classmates and more recent advisees in this group. I worked for a year on a project that did not go anywhere.

Second, the opposite scenario occurs if students enter a graduate program with a topic already firmly in mind and cannot be swayed by new knowledge from the literature or from course work and guidance. The shock in this case occurs when they discover late in the game that the topic might not work out and—with little time left—they will have to let it go and rush to find a new one, or let the original idea change and develop in ways they do not like. In this second scenario, a topic may not work because it isn't a researchable dissertation project (e.g., there aren't any real questions). Another reason is that there may be no advisers interested in or knowledgeable about students' pre-existing topics that already seem written in stone. A third reason might be that such students already seem to know the answers to the questions they are asking. In this case, real research is not possible.

Here are two stories to exemplify some of these problems. Both stories are about Japanese women that I was advising at the time, tenured mid-career teachers working full time (up to six days a week) and studying in an American university doctoral program in Japan. I recount them with permission from them.

Story 1: Eriko (pseudonym)

> Even after all her course work, Eriko had no idea what to research and write about for her dissertation. Or I should say that she had numerous ideas—most stemming from small interactions and issues concerning the students in her pre-service teacher education classes and one from a volunteer class in which she taught English to elderly Japanese people. She was an empathetic teacher and wanted to document the extraordinary stories of a few of her students. Within a two-year (plus) period, starting at the end of her course work, she went through perhaps four main topics, did some reading on each one, discussed them all with me in writing and in-person. But in all cases, I could find no core issue that could be explored in a dissertation-length project (this will be the length of a book, I told her!). Why do elderly people study English? How will my blind student survive in his teacher preparation course? How do my students choose a topic for their final research paper? What experiences do they have in their fourth year practicum? I could imagine all of these as short projects, perhaps appropriate for a master's thesis, but none as a doctoral dissertation in our particular program. One reason was that she already knew the answers to some of her

questions, and another was that she was not sure how to turn her interests into truly researchable questions.

Eriko went around and around, meanwhile reading in the literature of teacher preparation, reflection, and (eventually) teacher identity and "possible selves" (Markus & Nurius, 1986; Dörnyei, 2009, cited in Eriko's work). During her sabbatical, she spent the first several months doing nothing but searching for literature in these areas, reading, and writing response journal entries. After many written and oral discussions with me, she began to see how ideas and readings were beginning to gel. She was beginning to understand that her dissertation would be the equivalent of seven or eight 30–40 page course papers. She was developing some expertise in the topic of teacher preparation and in the conceptual background of possible selves as a result of her reading, her response journals, and her discussions with me and with a classmate. I began to get research memos from her that had a focus, that were coherent, and that above all were interesting to both her and me and that expressed ideas with staying power. At this point, everything seemed to come together rather quickly and she settled on a topic that used possible selves theory to document the year-long changes in and reflections on identity of the students in her fourth year teacher education seminar as they went through a short teaching practicum and wrote a final graduation paper. But it took a sabbatical and nearly two years of mulling, reading, talking, and memo writing and 11 shifts of topic. I counted.

Story 2: Ryoko (pseudonym)

Nearly two years before she finally settled on a topic, Ryoko was convinced about what she wanted to do: Learn why more English teachers in Japan did not teach about gender issues in the EFL class. Ryoko had been an avid feminist since her time years before in a women's studies MA program in the United States. In our many conversations over two years, she explained to me repeatedly that teachers *should* be teaching gender issues (among other sociopolitical issues), and that not doing so indicated a problem with the teachers or with the curriculum. In essence, she wanted to ask teachers the following loaded question: Why don't you teach gender issues in your class? One of the goals of her project would be to convince them to do so. I finally had to say quite directly that this topic—one that would put participants on the defensive by asking *why (not)* questions and then trying to tell EFL teachers what they should be doing—would not work for a dissertation. She needed to start with a question or curiosity about which she did not have all the answers, not with a moralistic stance about what she thought teachers should be doing. She also would get nowhere with a research question that confronted teachers in interviews and class observations with her own beliefs about feminist principles.

We went around and around. We talked, in person and by email. I read a couple of Ryoko's previous writings on feminist language teaching. I asked her to write (and revise, and re-write, and re-think) purpose statements: "The purpose of my research is to . . . ." But she seemed stuck. She seemed to **already know** what stances and content EFL teachers should be using in their English classes in Japan. I saw passion in her topic idea and the possibilities for lifelong career interests, but no possibility for real research on questions for which she already had answers.

I finally asked what she thought about trying to identify avowedly feminist teachers (thus avoiding the *should*-stance), and asking them about their histories, beliefs, and classroom practices. I suggested *how* questions, not *why* questions (Becker, 1998; Silverman & Marvasti, 2008). Such an approach would not put participants on the defensive or require that she

tell anyone what she thought they should be doing, either
explicitly or implicitly. She could start with genuine questions,
about how the selected teachers had arrived at their beliefs
(interviews and journals), and how or whether they enacted
their beliefs in actual classroom practice (observations,
handouts, and any published descriptions of their teaching).
Overnight Ryoko had a breakthrough and the project took
off from that point. But getting there took many many
months, and, as in the case of Eriko, a sabbatical.

In these two cases, I was able to think along with the students, but I could not tell them what to do or force them to make
decisions before they were ready. I could not shorten the reading
and thinking time either. I could only be a sounding board, guide
them to some resources, and help them understand what a dissertation was (and was not). These cases are not unusual, I think.
In all cases, students need long-term careful guidance as they are
going through a topic-construction process, either because they
are quite lost about what to do research on, or because they have
been too firmly wedded from the beginning to a particular idea
that cannot be turned into a dissertation project that is suitable
or that has staying power. But another common problem in topic
construction is that such early long-term guidance is quite rare.
Professors and advisers (assuming students have latched on to
someone compatible and interested) might not be willing or able
to make time to think along with students at early stages. Students,
on the other hand, might not be able to make time to work with
the needed focus and intensity because of full-time work responsibilities (as in the cases of Eriko and Ryoko, who found their way
into their projects only during year-long sabbaticals). And after
course work, students tend to be quite isolated; if they live far
from campus, it is difficult for them to form study groups so they
can consult with each other. In these cases, advisers and students
need to recognize the challenges, and not give up too quickly.

☞ Where Ideas for Topics Come From

A lot of ideas that help students construct dissertation topics come from readings. I talk about this later in a chapter on reading (Chapter 5). However, as I draft the current chapter, I am trying to come up with a single example of someone I know who did a doctoral dissertation that was not personally connected with something in his or her life. I can't come up with any examples. The first time I became aware of this was in the first or second year in my own doctoral program and I learned about the dissertation topics of a few classmates who were ahead of me. One Japanese woman wrote a dissertation on English phonology, as a way to understand and improve her own poor pronunciation in English. A man who was deeply involved in a gay relationship wanted to write a life history of his partner. And me, I eventually wanted to find out how writing in a graduate program transformed people's identities, starting with my own. So even though I did not write about myself in my dissertation, my interest started with curiosities about my own situation.

The doctoral students that I have been working with in recent years are all teachers, mostly of English as a foreign language (EFL) or of teacher preparation courses in the Japanese system. They are immersed in classroom contexts and deal constantly with questions of teaching methods, learning and beliefs about learning, second language acquisition, anxiety, motivation, testing and assessment, student change over time, and teacher beliefs and interactions with students. They are also interested in their own intellectual and professional development and those of their teacher colleagues. Their dissertation topics almost always have emerged out of their own work activities, even if they do not study their own classes.

However, if we look to our own classes or our own lives for possible dissertation topics, it will be tempting to investigate something so familiar that we cannot generate genuine questions or curiosities about it. We are blind to oddities. Familiar routines and patterns in our work and personal lives help us survive, of course. People cannot live in a constant state of uncertainty and questioning. But the dissertation topic that works needs to find some real questions (gaps, mysteries, puzzles) amidst the familiarity. Otherwise, we have no reason to do real research. So the question for future dissertation writers is, what can they see in some aspect of their own work and lives that they really don't understand? Routines, familiar patterns, and expectations can obscure true puzzles.

Another source of topics might be linked to a future dissertation writer's political and ideological beliefs, as was the case for Ryoko. Commitment to social action or to community service or to understanding political and social structures and goals can be a starting place for some kinds of doctoral projects. The hazard here, as was the case with Ryoko, is that a topic that aims to change the world rather than inquire about the world might not suit a research-based dissertation. A dissertation writer who already believes she knows how the world works and what should be changed does not have an inquiring mind. She has answers, not questions.

In this era of globalization and cross-cultural interaction, topics can also emerge as doctoral students cross cultures and attempt to make a life studying and working in unfamiliar places (I include native English speakers working outside their home countries). Such students understandably want to pursue a topic that might lead to work possibilities. Many international students in doctoral programs outside their home countries or in universities where they must study in their second languages are in this situation. The study of linguistic and cultural adjustments over time, of identity and survival, starting with the self, holds many genuine questions for future dissertation writers. On the topic of second language, I cannot imagine how some of my own students, second language users of English, can possibly do doctoral work and write book-length dissertations in their L2. Could I do this in my second languages (Spanish, French)? I can't imagine this, but thousands of students worldwide do it, and some of them study how they and others manage a life in an L2. The point is that one's own challenging work and linguistic situations can provide the starting place for dissertation topics.

☞ Constructing a Topic That Is Unique to You

Maybe *unique* is too strong a word for a dissertation topic, but the point is that some questions, experiences, ideas, and issues stem from something quite particular to yourself. With such a topic, a doctoral student has the opportunity to teach her professors and adviser something—a great position to be in. (Professors try to hide this, but they can sometimes be bored by students' topics if they feel they are not learning anything.) One of my former doctoral students, Hanako Okada, who suggested this idea to me, constructed a topic that built upon a set of experiences she had had since childhood that were quite particular to her. She had been a Japanese international student in Europe as a child, where her father was posted for business, and all her life had attended only international schools in the medium of English, rather than Japanese schools. She continued in international schools when her family returned to Japan. So without ever living in an English-dominant country, she became a bilingual user of both English and Japanese. Her childhood experiences, through high school, prompted her curiosity about the rather odd "hybrid" identities of high school students in Japanese international schools, where English was the medium of instruction. This curiosity, closely tied to her own experiences, led to a complex qualitative case study of the experiences and identities of several international high school students in Japan (Okada, 2009).

One other example (from many) of a doctoral student who capitalized on her own unique situation, is that of Youngjoo Yi, who was an international doctoral student in the midwest of the United States. As a Korean tied closely to the local Korean community, she had access to a fascinating and understudied group: Korean adolescents who were carving out identities and literacy skills in Korean and English in their online literacy activities (Yi, 2005a, 2005b, 2013). Yi not only had the bilingual skills needed to pursue such a topic, but she also had training and experience as a secondary school teacher so knew well that she would enjoy working with adolescent language learners. The topic was such a rich one for her that it led to many post-dissertation publications and subsequent job opportunities in U.S. universities.

In both these cases, the two doctoral students relied heavily on their bilingual statuses (as native speakers of Japanese and Korean) to do research that a monolingual English user could never do, and on their insider connections to local and specialized communities.

In sum, it pays to spend some time reflecting on your own life experiences to see what puzzles, problems, talents, and linguistic and cultural resources might lie there that could be developed into a dissertation topic that no one else could do.

☞ Choosing a Quantitative, Mixed-Method, or Qualitative Approach That Fits Your Topic

Many guidebooks insist that the research questions developed early in a study must guide the choice of methodological approach. This is true to a great extent. If you are curious about test scores of students who are taught by different methods, then it is likely you will select a method that allows you to compare and analyze sets of test scores in the form of numbers. You might also have in mind some questions about groups of people that require large-scale surveys. In such cases, you would hope to be guided by a good questionnaire designer and statistician for an adviser and to have taken (and enjoyed and passed) your statistics courses. If you are interested in finding out how people change over time (identities, knowledge, beliefs), you might use qualitative techniques to find out what people say about themselves and their experiences (interviews, journals, email conversations with you), and possibly a quantitatively analyzed questionnaire about their beliefs (carefully constructed and validated first). Or you might have questions about people's life stories, their experiences over time, or the life of a community that require extensive conversations with individuals and detailed observations of them in their own settings. A qualitative (ethnographically inspired or narrative) approach might suit your questions.

That said, there are also people who really love numbers and the precision of controlled (quasi)experiments and analyses. Such a person should not set about doing a messy qualitative study of people's lives and will likely be attracted to topics involving experiments, comparisons, surveys, and existing data bases. Others really hate numbers and counting and statistical analyses, and either did not study much math or statistics in their lives, or did and failed to become interested or proficient. But other people simply believe that some things just can't be counted and that it is the uncountable messy things in life that they are really interested in. Plan ahead if you are in this latter group because you might find yourself committing to a long and complex dissertation process, one that could be fascinating but seemingly endless. (*Note:* A seemingly endless dissertation topic can morph into one's life work.)

And if you are a nonnative speaker of English interested in pursuing a qualitative research project but fear that you won't be able to write well enough, take heart. You will indeed be able to write up a qualitative project (see Belcher & Hirvela, 2005, on this important issue), as many of my own students have successfully done. The trick is not to be deceived into believing that native English speakers can write well just because they are native speakers, and not to compare your drafts with anyone's finished pieces of writing. (It makes no sense to compare your early draft with the published 20th draft of someone else.) It is equally important to trust your evolving expertise in your topic knowledge and your intellectual skills, which might turn out to be more important than your English proficiency (Chang & Kanno, 2010). You will be happy in the end that you didn't select an easier topic for yourself (i.e., one that involves less writing); boredom with the wrong topic will be much harder to deal with than will writing and revising. It helps to write constantly, of course (see Chapter 3 on writing research memos and journals), and as your writing skills develop, you might even find yourself enjoying the fascinating and complex process of turning difficult ideas into lines of words (Casanave & Sosa, 2008).

The point is: Don't embark on a methodological approach that you are likely to hate. Try to figure this out early in your doctoral program. It will also be beneficial to identify an adviser who is philosophically compatible with you ("life is messy; there is no truth" versus "aspects of life can be objectified and examined with scientific precision") and who can guide your development as a quantitative, qualitative, or mixed-method researcher. Opinions differ, by the way, about mixed-method research. On the one hand, supporters urge us to be pragmatic and do what works (Johnson & Onwuegbuzie, 2004; Teddlie & Tashakkori, 2009), and some skeptics find that qualitative approaches such as case studies are amenable to mixed methods (Hesse-Biber, 2010). Others say that it is difficult for researchers to become true experts in more than one approach, and that philosophical and epistemological differences make the mixing of philosophically incompatible methods questionable (see the discussion in Guba & Lincoln, 2005).

☞ Issues of Access, Consent, and IRB Approval

Once you have an idea of some areas of interest for a possible dissertation topic, it is a good idea to consider earlier rather than later whether you might have any problems getting access to the participants and sites you might want to investigate, and whether it might be a problem getting participants to sign an official consent-to-participate-in-research form. Even if you don't recruit actual participants until later, it is possible to predict whether you might have problems. However, don't give up if you have problems getting access; get advice from others, be strategic, and (important) follow ethical guidelines.

For instance, consider Hanako Okada's (2009) study of Japanese high school students in international schools in Tokyo, mentioned above. Not only did she need consent from the principals of the schools where she did observations and interviews, she also needed consent from the students, *and from their parents*, because the students were underage. She had to convince all parties that her research would do no harm to the school or the students and that it might in fact benefit them in some way. Finding institutions and people that are willing to participate and to sign actual consent forms can take many months. If some institutions and people refuse to participate, will you have a Plan B ready and time to pursue it?

Another major hurdle, later in the dissertation planning process, happens at universities where doctoral students must submit their research plans to a university review board for human subjects IRB (Institutional Review Board) approval. If you are not familiar with this procedure, check with your university and look the procedures up on the Internet early in your doctoral program so that you know what to expect later on. This is an ethical requirement in many universities. You will need to write a plan of your research and indicate clearly how you will protect the human participants you plan to work with—their anonymity, their safety, their reputations, their well-being. You might even need to take an online course demonstrating that you understand ethical guidelines. The details of your plan will be written after you have some clear ideas for a topic, but it is a good idea from the beginning to envision the IRB committee looking over your shoulder.

☞ Issues of Multiple Languages

In the early stages of topic construction, it is likely that you will already know whether you want to collect data in more than one language and from more than one cultural group, and whether your own language skills are adequate for a multilingual project. The challenge goes both ways: If your L1 is English, and your dissertation topic requires you to collect data from native speakers of a non-English language, you will either need to find participants who are very advanced users of English (so you can collect data in your L1, not theirs) or to collect data in your participants' native languages. In this latter case, you will need to be a bilingual user of your participants' L1s to be able to prepare materials, comprehend data, and translate to English later, or to bring in a research assistant who can do your data collection and translation for you. If you are an L2 user of English collecting data from native English speakers, you have the same problem in reverse. If you are an L2 user of English collecting data in your mother tongue, you are then faced with the problem of translating your data and your instruments (surveys, interview questions, etc.) to English for presentation later in the dissertation. In all cases, issues of translation can get quite messy (Temple, 1997; Temple & Young, 2004). If you are not a skilled (and trained) translator or a balanced bilingual, then plan to get some help from a professional later.

Ideally, multilingual-multicultural research is done in teams of people with multiple language skills and cultural expertise.

But doctoral dissertations are nearly always the work of a single individual who is supposed to demonstrate autonomy and independence (a mythical goal as I mention in Chapter 8). Plan early, in the topic construction stage, for how you might handle multiple language and culture issues. In all cases, I urge students of all language backgrounds to get their multilingual data checked, at least in part, by someone else.

☞ Your Role in Your Topic

Traditionally, in research in the positivist scientific tradition, the researcher-author is invisible in a final research report. Graduate students learn early on, by imitating (often poorly written; Billig, 2013) published writing or by following instructions by professors and guidebooks, to eliminate themselves from their reports. They overuse the passive voice, refuse to use first-person pronouns, do not describe who they are and why they were motivated to do a particular project, and do not locate themselves in their own research. I have even seen research reports in which an author who is researching a class that he himself is teaching refers to himself in the third person to hide the fact that he is centrally located in his own project. In general, many novice academic writers mistakenly believe that any reference to themselves constitutes a kind of biased subjectivity that is to be avoided rather than acknowledged and incorporated.

However, guidelines such as those published in the APA manual and other guide books on writing ask authors to report their roles in their research openly, to tell readers who they are and why they are interested in their topic, and to use first person to describe what they did (American Psychological Association, 2009; Becker, 1986; Smagorinsky, 2011). From his Vygotskian perspective, Smagorinsky (2011) described some of his frustrations as a reviewer of journal manuscripts when he could not understand who the authors were in relation to a project nor could he picture the contexts in which the research took place. As a result, readers could not fully comprehend or trust the findings of the research.

You will polish the details of style much later in the dissertation process. However, at the earliest stages, plan on locating yourself honestly and openly in your dissertation project, describing your interests and motivations in doing the project and, where appropriate, referring to yourself in first person. (See further comments in Chapter 9.)

Summary of Main Points in This Chapter

1. Constructing a researchable topic takes a long time and should be started early.

2. Most doctoral project topics start from a student's own life experiences and interests.

3. A topic that works needs to be substantial enough to turn into a book-length report, to have staying power, and to address questions for which the student has no clear answers.

4. Choice of methods for investigating a topic needs to suit both the research questions and the researcher's personal preferences.

5. Getting access to research sites and permission from individual participants can be difficult and needs to be considered early in the topic construction process.

6. Constructing a topic for research in more than one language and culture is an asset that bilingual doctoral students can bring to a project. However, data collection and translation issues can add complications later.

7. Students have a role in their own research projects, including a clear and honest presence in the write-up of the dissertation.

☞ Suggestions for Discussion and Reflection ☜

1. What aspects of your life interest you deeply, either because of work that you are doing or experiences you have had? What puzzles and questions do you have about these aspects of your life that might be turned into research questions?

2. Whom do you relate to more in the two stories in this chapter, Eriko or Ryoko? Write a personal statement about your style of constructing a dissertation topic, and an evaluation or critique of your actual or planned strategies.

3. In a dissertation journal entry and/or a conversation with a colleague, discuss what topics of interest could be studied in a long-term book length project. What qualities or features do you think lend themselves to a dissertation-length project as opposed to a course paper or a journal article?

4. What kinds of dissertation topics do you think might be difficult or impossible to carry out in a research project? Why?

Chapter 5

Reading in the Early Stages

From my own experience and that of my students, I have found that other than actually writing a doctoral dissertation, reading in preparation for it is probably the most time-consuming activity in the dissertation journey. It *cannot* wait until the last minute—i.e., until you have to start writing a literature review. Reading is slow and needs to start well before this point and continue throughout the early design and writing stages. You will need to read a lot whether you are doing a quantitative or qualitative study, not only to build your own knowledge of the theoretical and empirical work that has already been done in your area of interest, but also to get a clear sense of how your own project will fit and contribute. This includes knowing about other dissertations that have been written in your area of interest.

Not many studies have been conducted on reading in the early stages of a doctoral program, but Kwan's study of 16 Hong Kong–based Chinese doctoral students (2008, 2009) is one that has shown that "choices of crucial reading can be shaped by issues that emerged from the processes of researching and thesis-writing" (Kwan, 2009, p. 181). Kwan found in particular that the reading done for early pieces of writing (pilot studies, proposals, qualifying exams) was essential to help these doctoral students prepare for actual thesis writing. As I discuss in this chapter, early reading can help you find your topic; later reading can help you refine and focus it. In all cases, reading helps you develop expertise in your area of interest.

However, some academic reading can be notoriously tedious (pretentious, overly complex, boring, impersonal; see Billig, 2013; Caulley, 2008; Richardson & St. Pierre, 2005). You will soon get a sense of this when you find that it is easier to get through some readings than others. Are you falling asleep while you read? Rolling your eyes in frustration? Or looking forward to turning to the next page? Regardless of the kind of reading, some people are incredibly fast readers and seem to fly through articles and books in no time, but I have not met many people like this, even if they are reading in their first language. I am not a fast reader, either. Although I seem to be reading something all the time, my pace is slow unless the reading is unusually accessible, well-written, and interesting. (Try finding many such readings in academia!) I also find that it takes me time to become familiar with each writer's style. And even though I know that I don't need to read every word, it continues to be tempting to do so. I am also the kind of reader who needs to re-read important articles and books. I just can't seem to get everything I need in just one reading, even though I am reading in my native language. I have also found that when I go back to important older readings, I get something new every time. In short, because reading for the dissertation is so time-consuming, especially if students are reading in their second languages, it needs to be started early, and continued up until the time that serious writing begins (at which point it can be a distraction if we can't make ourselves stop).

Given the importance of reading in dissertation work, I was surprised in reading Silverman and Marvasti's (2008) book on doing qualitative research to find no chapter on reading and only one entry on reading in the index. This referred readers to a page and a half of their 550-page book on why it is important to keep a record of readings. Perhaps the authors assume that by the time readers pick up this book, their reading has already been completed. Other books and articles on reading as part of the research process deal with the literature review, usually referring to the writing of the review, without much on the reading in preparation for it (Feak & Swales, 2009; Ridley, 2008; Swales & Lindemann 2002). Murray and Beglar (2009), on the other hand, have a full (if fairly prescriptive) chapter on "preparing to write" that includes advice about reading and useful information about locating sources.

All scholars need to read as part of exploring new topics. However, a surprise for novice researchers is that some senior academics find themselves too busy to read much at all for their research and writing and instead rely on existing reviews or on help from graduate assistants, who do the reading and summarizing for them (Shirley Dex interview, in Carnell et al., 2008, p. 99). I was surprised to discover that this is an apparently normal practice among some faculty.

In short, I suggest reading efficiently and strategically as part of doctoral dissertation work and doing your own reading. This might mean not reading every word of everything you find, but at least consulting primary and secondary sources yourself.

☞ Reading A Lot, or Not, Early in the Dissertation Journey

Although opinions differ, intensive and extensive reading seems essential for doctoral students who are starting to plan dissertations and who may not yet be familiar with what has been written on their topics or who the central figures are in certain research areas. It is not just a matter of learning what is what, but who is who. Reading helps guide all novice researchers in developing this knowledge of a (sub)field and its contributors. Reading later in the dissertation journey becomes intimately connected to fieldwork and is guided by actual research experiences rather than by searches of data bases (Kwan, 2009; Wolcott, 2001).

That said, here are two excerpts from one of my own dissertation journals (see Chapter 3 on different kinds of reflective writing), written in 1987 and 1988, separated by one year, before I had gotten deeply involved in actual data collection, analysis, or writing. I found myself depressed and deflated when I read some important published articles that showed that my ideas had already been thought of and my potential study already done. The second excerpt also shows how key published work led me to other useful sources, and gave me some hints about what I wanted and did not want to do, in spite of my continued frustration.

Dissertation Journal Book 1:

> [A friend] gave me manuscript copies of McCarthy and Berkenkotter & Huckin, both to appear in RTE [*Research in the Teaching of English*], both what I'm doing. I feel suddenly

deflated. I thought I had arrived at something somewhat original. Here it is already, even phrased as I have phrased my thoughts. (p. 6)

The Berkenkotter, Huckin, & Ackerman piece came out in *RTE*. Reread it, and much I could have written. I believe it was they (among others) who directed me to the work in the sociology of science. So their underpinnings, their motivation, some of their questions are the same as mine. [. . .] Back to Herrington again. I just couldn't handle her analytic schemes. 5000 of them with big fancy words from Aristotle. Shit. What is it I want to know? (pp. 230–231)

As I said, even though I was depressed about this at the time, I was glad to have discovered published work directly relevant to my own evolving ideas early in my dissertation planning process. Having discovered it, and other relevant readings early, I was able to work them into my dissertation proposal and get a sense of how my own vague ideas for a study were situated in a compatible and focused body of work. I also saw certain key readings as models for conceptual frameworks and for case study and qualitative methods. And once I had recovered from the discovery that my own ideas were not original, I was comforted to realize that if some well-known published authors were writing on such topics, then the topics, and my own, must be important and could lead to offshoots and variations.

Some faculty and advisers might take the position that reading should come later, after doctoral students have worked out their own ideas. Too much reading, some people think, can intimidate (novice) researchers who might lack confidence in their own inchoate ideas. A long time ago, sociologist Robert Merton (1967) discussed the problem of reading too much because he (citing Comte) feared it messed up one's brain for one's own project. Here is an excerpt from my dissertation journal that I wrote after rereading Merton:

> *Dissertation Journal Book 2:*
>
>> Rereading Merton (1967), *On Theoretical Sociology.* [...] Great quote about Comte about the value (or lack of) of knowing what predecessors have done. Comte refers to "cerebral hygiene" as the principle of washing one's mind "clean of everything but his own ideas by the simple tactic of not reading anything even remotely germane to his subject" (Merton, p. 33). Merton then quotes Comte: "The cerebral hygiene is exceedingly salutary to me, particularly in order to maintain the originality of my peculiar meditations" (Merton, 1967, pp. 33–34). "Tension between erudition and originality." Merton concludes with a discussion of how the classics function in the work and thinking of sociologists. Very interesting. (pp. 47–48)

This view, that too much reading can be harmful, that "cerebral hygiene" rather than reading can assist with creativity, intrigued me then. I learned years later that Merton and Comte were not the only ones who doubted the value of too much reading. Anthropologist Harry Wolcott (2001), too, saw himself as a writer, not a reader. Here is a story quoted from Wolcott, who talked about his own complicated relationship with reading. He asked whether we consider ourselves basically readers or writers, and identifies himself as a writer:

> *Story: Harry Wolcott on his own relationship to reading and writing*
>
>> Do you consider yourself essentially a reader or essentially a writer? I recognize that my strict dichotomy may be little more than rationalization, for I do not consider myself a reader. That is not to suggest I do not read; rather, in

a professional community of readers (scholars, teachers, researchers, students), and speaking relatively, I am neither a voracious reader nor am I well read. [. . .] Most of my reading is professional, and most of my professional reading is tedious. I rarely read for pleasure, and I seldom read for relaxation.

I read what I must; I write whenever I can. That probably explains why I find field research so appealing: I become actively involved in the process, seeing and hearing and pondering everything firsthand rather than getting it passively and secondhand. [. . .] Not surprisingly, I regard my most effective reading as that done while I am engaged in fieldwork and/or preparing a manuscript. Writing gives purpose and focus to searching for new sources and reviewing old ones. It provides pegs on which to hang relevant ideas and a basis for deciding what to retain, what to let go. (Wolcott, 2001, pp. 21–22)

Although I agree with Wolcott about the value of writing to help focus one's reading, I am not personally comfortable avoiding reading myself at early stages of a project, or recommending that students practice "cerebral hygiene" of this type. One reason is that no matter how original students believe their ideas to be, it is highly likely that someone has thought of them before and that some people have already gotten famous writing about them. Note my discovery of this in Book 1 of my dissertation journals. I think I would prefer knowing this sooner rather than later in a research project. Plus, extensive early reading can provide students with ideas for topics, models for methods, and actual language and turns of phrases that can be "exploited" for use in their own work (Jan Blommaert interview, in Carnell et al., 2008, p. 89). Ultimately, early extensive reading serves to familiarize novice researchers with work and people in the field in time for them to use existing work in their own projects.

But, as is clear, opinions differ. Advisers and other professors may or may not have strong feelings about the value of early and extensive reading. Best to check with them.

⌒ Locating and Evaluating Materials

Searching for readings can be fun or tedious. Whichever attitude students take, searches take a long time, are multi-pronged, and increasingly electronic. They happen by author name, by title of readings, and by topic and key words. It is rare for doctoral students to begin their search for readings in a vacuum; there is always a starting place, through readings done in course work, suggestions from faculty, or chance discoveries made through browsing. But the search must be for real readings, primary as well as secondary sources, not cut-and-paste Wikipedia information. (But Wikipedia can provide interesting biographical information about well-known authors and clarification of confusing concepts!)

Students who are handed a reading list by their advisers are in a fortunate position in some ways, in that they have a head start. However, they miss the pleasures and discoveries of the search—the detective work, as it were. Still, searching on their own can turn up many essential readings but also a lot of extraneous materials whose relevance (or lack of) might not be obvious to the novice researcher. A good adviser can help here, by pointing students in promising directions and helping to identify key figures and readings. Library staff as well as faculty can help students identify appropriate electronic databases and print and electronic journals that the library subscribes to. With a few key articles and books in hand or downloaded, particularly recent ones, students can mine the reference lists and bibliographies for many more sources and either search for print copies or download them electronically through university library connections.

These days, of course, many useful (as well as useless) sources can be found with good key word searches on scholar.google or some other electronic database. Beware of key words that are too vague to locate focused articles and books, though if you are lucky, useful items will appear on the first page or two. Entering "academic writing," I find over three million sources, but the first ones are potentially useful to things I am interested in. "Academic writing in a second language" pulls up two and a half million sources, but again, the ones on the first couple of pages are sources I can use. The same problem can occur with many specialized databases—all students, therefore, need to develop strategies for selecting and evaluating sources found on the Internet. Libraries, advisers, faculty, and more experienced students can all help in this regard (see also Murray & Beglar, 2009, pp. 60–61).

If you attend conferences and go to sessions on topics of potential dissertation interest to you, you will be lucky if the presenter has a reference list to hand out. If not, presenters are often willing to send you references lists electronically, so be sure to introduce yourself to presenters who might be helpful to you in this way and may turn out to be good contacts down the line.

One thing to consider is that searching for readings (and the note-making that goes along with reading; see Chapter 3) needs to be individualized to suit each person. The high-tech/pure-tech strategy will suit some doctoral students and not others, and strategies will change with time and purpose. One of my favorite strategies is to locate a few relevant and recent sources, and then let one name (author, title) lead to another (and another and another). Eventually the same names begin cropping up, and I get a sense of who is who in an area of inquiry. But my collection strategies have changed over the years as my small house has filled up with more papers and books than I can wade through. I have always loved paper copies of everything for many reasons, including my ability to pencil comments and underlinings directly onto the text. But I can no longer manage more paper. So I access books through the library if possible and fill my computer with downloaded files or articles in a couple of broadly categorized file folders. The articles are conveniently alphabetized by author (I title each file with author's last name, year of publication, and a few key words from the title). To avoid accumulating more paper, I am forced to read from the computer screen, which I hate, and to use mark and annotate tools if I want to highlight anything. It's not the same as paper.

⌢ Conceptual vs. Empirical Readings

As students no doubt know from course work or previous experience in a master's program, many kinds of readings support graduate work. Basic information can be gathered from textbooks and sites on the Internet such as Wikipedia. However, such sources are rarely used for doctoral dissertation work. Instead, students are expected to rely on professional books and monographs, articles reporting research, conceptual works (e.g., articles on theory or philosophical perspectives), completed dissertations by others, and less often articles and books on pedagogy. For a research degree like the PhD, students are expected to know the research literature in their areas of interest and to access conceptual and empirical sources with reputable academic standing, such as publications in refereed journals (i.e., articles and books that have gone through a peer-review process and been evaluated as worthy of publication). They are also expected to know some of the common conceptual and theoretical works that are used to frame studies.

Thousands of print and online academic journals (i.e., periodicals, not records of daily experience; see Chapter 3) now exist, some featuring conceptual or theoretical works and many emphasizing empirical research. Increasingly, the journals themselves are rated and ranked (look up "impact factor"—a citation metric—on Wikipedia). Faculty can help students identify journals and academic book publishers that have good reputations and help them identify important conceptual and empirical works. This is not to deny the importance of less well-known, more local journals, but to alert students to the reputation factor of different publications. With time and guidance, students will be able to identify the main journals in their areas of interest and the central figures that have helped shape a field. These central figures, theorists and researchers from the past and present, are the ones whose names appear frequently in highly ranked journals and as citations in the work of others and that deserve to be read by students and cited in their own work, along with other important, if lesser known, authors.

Some books and articles discuss and explore ideas. These are conceptual or theoretical works that make interesting reading for some people and boring reading for people who want to know only "what happened" in a study. Some conceptual works actually support their theories with the authors' original research, but the works themselves tend to be remembered less for the research than for the concepts and theories. In my own fields of interest, this is the case for past and present scholars such as Vygotsky, Bakhtin, Goffman, Foucault, Bourdieu, Lave and Wenger, and Engeström, among others. The value of such conceptual works is that a richly conceptualized theory can apply beyond the case of the original research and be adapted to new settings and purposes. Lave and Wenger (1991), for example, did research on midwives and butchers, among others, to develop their concept of Legitimate Peripheral Participation. Wenger's (1998) ideas on Communities of Practice stemmed from a study of insurance agents. Bakhtin was a literary critic and studied novels. Vygotsky was a child psychologist who studied cognitive development in young children. Goffman studied townspeople in the Shetland Islands and gamblers in Las Vegas. All these empirically supported theoretical works are cited frequently in social science fields that have little to do with the original research.

In addition to conceptual readings, empirical studies are essential reading for a doctoral dissertation—those based on actual research (gathered through observations, experiments, interviews, surveys, and documents) or on published reviews of existing research (review articles). The point of this kind of reading is to learn what other scholars have actually done, how they have done it (their methods), and what they have found (their findings). If such articles contain sufficient details, doctoral students can learn many things that might be useful for their own dissertation work: types of research designs, types of data, methods of collection, analytical schemes, and strengths and limitations of different kinds of studies. Such articles can also be models (good or bad) for how to frame a study conceptually, and how to discuss and interpret findings (always a difficult stage of the dissertation process). Perhaps most important in the early stages of dissertation planning is to learn what other researchers have done and how students' own studies might fit into and build on existing empirical work.

In making reading notes, it is helpful to distinguish between conceptual and theoretical works on the one hand and empirical studies on the other. Every dissertation will contain both ideas (concepts, theories) and data (empirical elements). It is also helpful to learn early in the doctoral program what you as a dissertation writer are interested in: Some people are fascinated by theory and can't get enough of it. Others want only to get to the pragmatic job of learning about existing research and then starting their own project. If you are forced to read outside your comfort area and area of interest, be patient, and try to find a balance. Negative and positive reactions, explained with reasons, make for wonderful entries in a reading response journal or in other personal ways of keeping track of readings (see Chapter 3).

⌒ Thinking Ahead to a Literature Review

In thinking ahead to a literature review, every dissertation writer needs to figure out how much reading is enough—first for the proposal and then later for the full dissertation, and then when to stop. There are some signs to pay attention to that will tell you that you have reached, or are reaching, the saturation point.

First is developing a sense of familiarity with ideas and studies you read about. You may find yourself thinking: I know this already, I've read about this before. This is a very good sign that you are developing expertise in an area.

Second, is the reappearance of some of the same names in citations and reference lists of your readings. As every novice dissertation writer has discovered, sometimes the same names are cited in many readings on your topic of interest. This is a sign that these frequently cited authors are important in the field and should probably be read in the original, not just as secondary citations. I urge dissertation writers not to take short cuts—read important works in the original (or translated original). Name recognition is also a sign that you are getting familiar with the important figures in your subfield.

Some guide books can help with the writing of literature reviews (Feak & Swales, 2009; Ridley, 2008). However, given that scholarly opinions differ as to the role and value of extensive versus focused literature reviews in doctoral dissertations (Boote & Beile, 2005, 2006; Maxwell, 2006), check closely with your adviser(s) as to what and how much he or she thinks you should be reading. But remember: Even though reading is essential, you will always feel like you can never know enough to be able to write a dissertation. You will need to constantly fight this insidious feeling that you lack of expertise and need to read just one more thing. And guess what: Your own professors are equally aware of their own incomplete knowledge. One reason they stay in academic life is to be able to be paid to continue learning.

Summary of Main Points in This Chapter

1. Effective reading lies at the heart of early dissertation work.

2. Opinions differ as to whether doctoral students and other scholars should read everything they can find or narrowly and judiciously. Should "cerebral hygiene" refer to a brain that is empty or full of readings?

3. Many techniques exist for locating resource materials—they need to suit each doctoral student and be honed and adapted as students become more skilled at searching. The same goes for methods of keeping track of readings (cf. Chapter 3).

4. Two basic kinds of readings can usefully be distinguished: conceptual readings (those that focus on ideas, theories, and discussions) and empirical readings (reports of actual research or reviews of actual research).

5. The trap of reading is that it is difficult to stop. It is possible to know when you have read enough for a particular project when ideas and names and types of studies become familiar. However, even if readers feel that a saturation point has not been reached, reading has to slow down or stop once the dissertation writing has begun. More reading will always be there waiting for you.

☞ Suggestions for Discussion and Reflection ☜

1. What are your own views, and those of classmates and faculty you know, about the value of maximizing or minimizing the amount of reading that researchers should do before beginning a project? What are the advantages of a brain that is full or empty of readings?

2. What techniques have you used to locate reading materials for your dissertation project? What techniques have been most and least successful for you? What ideas can you get from others about locating materials that you would like to try?

3. What are some of the most important conceptual-theoretical reading materials that you have found or that you know of and plan to read? What empirical studies have provided inspiration and models for your own ideas for research? What empirical studies have demonstrated what you really *don't* want to do? In each of these cases, what are the reasons for your assessments?

4. How do you think you will know when you have read enough to begin your actual dissertation work?

Chapter 6

Thinking Theoretically and Conceptually

┌─── MYTH #6 ────────────────────────────────

Theory plays an essential and elevated role in doctoral work.

> Maybe. But there is no need to fear theory. The word
> *theory* needlessly intimidates some people because they
> don't understand that a theory for most of our purposes
> is just an idea about how some phenomena or ideas or
> concepts relate to each other. We all think theoretically
> in our daily lives.

I recall that early in my doctoral program I was struck
by, and resistant to, the need to suddenly start thinking about
and discussing theory. I had just come from many years of ESL
teaching, and my work and the few publications I had done and
would do in my first few years of the program were very practical.
In fact, the only language teaching textbooks I ever wrote were
done during those theory-resistant years. Theory seemed margin-

ally connected to the issues I was interested in and the work I presumed I would be doing later. My disaffection with theory was not helped by my being forced to read theoretical works for classes (or empirical works grounded in theories) that seemed to me pretentious, long-winded, and sometimes just incomprehensible. I could not figure out why scholars in the social sciences—a collection of disciplines that study people, their communities, their education, and their interactions—needed to invent words and concepts that normal people had never heard of just to talk about ideas that everyone knew were common sense.

Debates between (post)positivists and qualitative inquirers were in full swing in the early and mid-1980s, and among other influential publications, some of us read Thomas Kuhn's (1970) *The Structure of Scientific Revolutions*. I was quite taken with that book at the time, which helped me think about science in new ways. I became puzzled and curious about facts and theories and paradigms. The distinction among them no longer seemed so clear cut. A footnote in Kuhn's book led me to a much earlier book that Kuhn (in tiny print) acknowledged had influenced him, Ludwig Fleck's (1935/1979) *The Genesis of a Scientific Fact*. The final dismantling of my naïve view of facts, reality, and theories occurred after I read Berger and Luckmann's (1966) *The Social Construction of Reality*. Things were not so simple, it seemed. Facts did not exist out there in some objective world awaiting to be discovered. They were constructed and agreed upon by communities of like-minded people and laden with theory. What a fascinating idea.

I am still not good at doing theory and, like most people, my ideas have changed over time and continue to do so. Lately I have been thinking about Maxwell's (2012) "realist approach" to qualitative inquiry, a critical response to what he sees as an extreme social constructionist position (Denzin & Lincoln, 2000). In general, I am more attracted than in the past to the ideas that underlie and frame the research we do. I see them as ways to frame my thinking about particular questions and observations and to make connections to other studies. I recognize that when I think about "assumptions" about a project I am working on that I am in some sense thinking theoretically. When I ask, "What are these data an example of?" or "What is this process or activity an example of?" I am asking about a concept. And when I ask, "What are the connections between this concept and another one?" I am asking a theoretical question.

Assumptions, beliefs, ideas, concepts, and theories all share some characteristics, the most salient of which is a level of abstraction that goes beyond the concrete details of our lives. All of us can recognize our assumptions, beliefs, and ideas, and we can probably come up with some examples of concepts in our daily lives. It is a short step from this kind of thinking to theoretical thinking: A theory makes clear how ideas or concepts are related. In this sense, it is a kind of model or network. This should not be an intimidating idea. Moreover, for most of the research that doctoral students do, we don't need "Grand Theory" or "Big T" theory (Marxism, Evolution, …) (Wolcott, 2001; a concept also used by Atkinson, 2010), but mid-level or commonsense theories that will help us think about and frame our work conceptually. We do this kind of thinking all the time in our everyday lives.

As much as researchers need some kind of theory or theories, theorizing can get out of hand, as has happened sometimes in disciplines such as sociology. I still smile when I read Howard Becker's (1998) critical comment about this, and I must admit that I share his own skepticism about the dangers of excessive abstraction in fields that are supposed to be about people:

> I have a deep suspicion of abstract sociological theorizing;
> I regard it as at best a necessary evil, something we need in
> order to get our work done but, at the same time, a tool that
> is likely to get out of hand, leading to a generalized discourse
> largely divorced from the day-to-day digging into social life
> that constitutes sociological science. (Becker, 1998, p. 4)

Anthropologist Harry Wolcott (2001) seems equally wary of the excessive devotion to formal theory by scholars who do fieldwork, including dissertation writers:

> I feel theory is overrated in terms of what most of us actually accomplish through our research. In theory-driven descriptive accounts, theory is more apt to get in the way than to point the way, to tell rather than ask what we have seen. [. . .]
>
> When and how theory makes its real entry into the research process is often masked by the canons of reporting. This is especially so in the constricted format of thesis and dissertation writing, in which the typically tedious review of the literature in a traditionally perfunctory second chapter includes an equally tedious recital of "relevant" theory. (Wolcott, 2001, pp. 186–187)

He reported asking his doctoral students to consider reviewing any needed literature and theories at the end of their dissertations instead of at the beginning, when data and findings make clear what is relevant and what needs to be connected to larger contexts and issues.

In spite of such dangers, major projects in a research-based doctoral program need some kind of theoretical foundation, even if just to be conceptualized in commonsense ways (Maxwell, 2005; Wolcott, 2005). Otherwise, we can't get a grasp of what the project is about in ways that will connect our work with other work in our fields.

In the remainder of this chapter, I expand on some of these ideas in the hope that by thinking about the various kinds of abstractions and framing you can do early in your doctoral program that the requirement to do so later won't be too overwhelming.

☞ Fear of Theory

There is *Theory* (capital T) and *theory* (small t), the former being formal and "grand" and the latter the middle-range theories that are more commonsense and accessible (Wolcott, 2001). Many of us feel intimidated by the notion of theory, imagining it to be the big T variety—abstract, formal, and inaccessible. We (I include myself here) are understandably anxious when we are told we need to frame our work theoretically or are asked at early stages of a doctoral project by someone in authority "What is your theory?" From doctoral studies onward, pressures to theorize our work might be heavier than in the past, when (in fields like anthropology, anyway) there was more interest in practical field-work. Wolcott (2001) recommends resisting such pressures:

> We must learn how to protect ourselves from being beaten down (or up) by insistence that every field study must be linked directly to theory. Theory is often employed as a sort of intellectual bludgeon, a killer-term used to menace problem-focused neophytes and belittle efforts at applied or "practical" research." (p. 183)

Theory, Wolcott continued, should be used to guide and clarify, not intimidate. And guidance and clarity are needed even for the most practical research project.

One reason for our anxiety is that theory is not something we can see concretely, in the way we can see our data. There is something comforting about the concreteness of data in that our senses are involved; we can see and sense things in an environment, observe people doing various activities in specific contexts, listen to what people say, read what they write, count their responses to surveys, collect and touch artifacts. Once we start to consider how all these concrete and visible things work together, and what they are examples of, we are thinking theoretically. But this is difficult to do at early stages of a doctoral project.

Theory can also be interesting in itself, and some people truly love immersing themselves in theory. Theory can be both challenging and intellectually stimulating. A small concern is that students can find themselves so intrigued by theoretical literature that they do not pay sufficient attention to the concrete stages of data collection and analysis. I am not sure how common this level of fascination with theory is among doctoral students, but I think it is more common for students to find the theoretical side of their doctoral projects intimidating, especially at first. In these latter cases, theory is particularly useful in helping us think about our research as we are doing it (Becker, 1998) and expanding what we can see beyond the concrete details of our study.

So we don't need to be fearful of theory—it is our sense of how some aspect of the world works. It grows out of the concrete data and practical interests that surround us (e.g., Becker, 1998; Maxwell, 2005) and extends how we view connections, interactions, and possibilities. In spite of occasional calls to "delink" theory and practice (Atkinson, 2010, p. 16), I find the theory-practice divide to be overblown and misleading.

☞ Contrasting Theorizing and Conceptualizing

In many discussions I have heard and read, the terms *theory* and *concept* are often used interchangeably. Both terms are common in every day parlance, and we use them unproblematically. I think it is useful, however, to distinguish them at least for purposes of researching and writing. Roughly, a concept is an abstract idea that develops from examples of data, and a theory is a model or network showing how concepts are related. Maxwell (2005,

p. 42) defines theory this way: "By 'theory,' I mean simply a set of concepts and the proposed relationships among these, a structure that is intended to represent or model something about the world. . . . The simplest form of theory consists of two concepts joined by a proposed relationship." Concepts and theories are thus maps of how some aspect of the world works; they further allow researchers to link their work to larger ideas and to the work of others.

It is possible that you don't need to worry about theory per se at all in your doctoral project but can refer instead to concepts and conceptual frameworks. If we hold that a theory is a formal portrayal of relationships among concepts and if a high level of abstraction and formality is not required in a doctoral dissertation, then we can work at a less formal level of theory or at the level of concepts. A concept is simply an idea that is an abstract representation of something quite concrete. By working at the level of concepts and conceptualizing, we remain closely tied to our data. As Becker (1998, p. 109) said: "My favorite way of developing concepts is in a continuous dialogue with empirical data" because "concepts are ways of summarizing data." In educational settings, for example, "learning" is a concept—it is abstract, it cannot be seen concretely because it resides inside people. But researchers can collect examples of what they think learning is and make inferences. "Let the case define the concept," Becker (1998, p. 123) said.

⌒ Finding and Using Theories and Concepts

As Yongyan Li and I pointed out from our own experiences and those with doctoral students (Casanave & Li, 2013), a common fear that novices have at early stages is that they need to find a theory or conceptual framework at the early stages of their doctoral projects in order to get started on a project. However, what they probably should be doing is thinking more empirically first, and then seeking ways to construct, rather than find, theories and concepts that can help frame their work. Constructing theories at the small t level, conceptualizing, as it were, evolves as researchers muck about in their plans, their readings, their fieldwork, and their actual data. It is almost impossible to find or construct an appropriate theory at earlier stages of a project even if readings provide possibilities, as I mentioned in the Fear of Theory section.

However, reading is a good way to get started on a search for theories and concepts, particularly if the reading is in the area(s) that doctoral students are working on and if it is interesting and accessible. I like to read published research articles to see how the authors frame their studies with theories or concepts and whether the frameworks actually help me understand their interpretations of their data and make connections to my own interests. One useful book for helping novice scholars understand how different qualitative research projects can be framed theoretically is Anfara and Mertz's (2006) edited book showcasing how different projects are framed. Each study in the book uses a different framework, and so provides a model for some of the possibilities. Reading textbooks on research methods might also be useful, as they usually include a chapter on theory or conceptual frameworks (e.g., Creswell, 2014, is quite prescriptive; Maxwell, 2005, is more exploratory). Reading articles and books on theory itself, even if they are difficult, can also provide students with ideas that can then be hashed over with classmates and professors.

Seeing data as examples of something can also productively lead to conceptual thinking. For instance, in education fields, teachers and researchers are inundated with pressures to use tests and test scores as concrete evidence of learning (learning must always be inferred from such second-hand evidence, of course). Test scores and test taking can thus be seen as examples and practices of concepts such as assessment, learning, and memory.

⌒ Framing

A frame around a picture holds it in place, keeps it within its boundaries, and helps viewers focus on what the artist intended. The function of a theoretical or conceptual frame is the same in a research project, where a frame is a more or less abstract idea that encircles a study. *Framing* as a verb refers to this activity of encircling a study with an idea that is larger and more abstract than the particular data you gather. It helps explain or justify why and how the study is being done, it focuses attention on what the researcher intends to study, and it helps researchers and readers interpret findings and connect them to other works and to larger ideas that can be "generalized."

Examples of framing will be evident in well-done empirical studies and will be discussed in books on research (in chapters that include phrases like *theoretical frameworks* or *conceptual frameworks*). A good adviser will discuss framing with you at the appropriate time, which could be earlier or later in the research project. Classmates as well will function as sounding boards for your ideas on framing.

But don't rush to frame your ideas for a dissertation project too soon. A conceptual frame that feels right at a very early stage, before data collection, might not seem appropriate later, after you have let your data help you conceptualize what the study is about. On the other hand, if you know from the beginning that you will model your own study on a project that has already been conducted and published (or appeared in dissertation form), then you might have a ready-made frame, or jumping-off place, constructed by someone else. In this case, you still need to read and study and discuss the primary sources for your frame.

☞ Avoiding Lip Service

As a reader of manuscripts submitted to journals for possible publication and also of many doctoral dissertation drafts, I see a lot of lip service paid to various concepts and theories, particularly those that are fashionable at the moment. Lip service is a kind of name dropping for the sake of demonstrating to an adviser or a manuscript reviewer that the writer is up-to-date on the latest faddish theories and knows the names of the theories' developers and main proponents (Billig, 2013). In such cases, it is usually quite obvious that the writers do not know much about the theories but feel obligated to mention them in order to appear knowledgeable.

However, it is quite difficult to become an expert in a full-blown formal theory or theoretical program, even after long years of study. Many well-known experts, for example, spend years trying to figure out what Vygotsky had to tell us, at the theoretical and conceptual levels, about children's cognitive development, and about how his unfinished ideas might be extended to new populations and contexts (Vygotsky died a long time ago, very young, and never fully developed his own theories). Many Vygotsky specialists refer to Wertsch's (1985, 1991) work, for example, but Wertsch himself does not know everything. Peter Smagorinsky (2011), for another, has tried to learn everything and would be considered an expert on Vygotsky by any of us, yet he admits that his knowledge is incomplete and that he continues to learn. James Lantolf is another who has studied Vygotsky and sociocultural theory for years (Lantolf & Thorne, 2006), and

Michael Cole (1996), editor of the journal *Mind, Culture, and Activity*, is yet another. They still don't know everything.

For a doctoral dissertation, no one expects you to become an expert in the many manifestations of the major theories in the social sciences. However, you need to have read enough primary and secondary sources to be able to discuss one or more theories somewhat intelligibly and to demonstrate that you understand the basic tenets of the theories you have chosen to help frame your study. This includes reading Vygotsky (or Bourdieu, or Lave and Wenger or whomever), not just reading *about* them. If concepts such as *zone of proximal development,* or *habitus,* or *legitimate peripheral participation* and *communities of practice* seem intriguing, then you'll need to read about them in the original (or in translation), and read as well what experts have to say about them (see Chapter 5 on reading). But beware of feeling compelled to trace back your "original" sources even further, a fascinating but potentially endless search (who did Vygotsky build his work on? Do you need to read Marx?). The point is: Be patient about the evolution of your knowledge.

⌒ Being Patient

I end this chapter with a story told by Christine Tardy about how she "came to terms with theory" only some years after her doctoral dissertation on genre knowledge had been completed (Tardy, 2010). Unlike many others, Tardy was interested in building theory, not just using it. I don't know if the development of her understanding could have progressed faster under different circumstances. But the point of the story is that the uncertainty and chaos at the beginning stages of a dissertation project are normal. We don't need to rush; our dissertations get finished even if our knowledge is incomplete. Our knowledge continues to grow long after a doctoral diploma is in hand. After all, all knowledge is incomplete. The following is a direct quote:

Story: Christine Tardy's understanding of theory, post-dissertation

> It is only in the past couple of years that I've come to view theory as less intimidating. I no longer see it solely as a "data-driven explanation" but instead as a kind of working knowledge. [. . .]
>
> The theory building process which I have shared here began, in one sense, with my teaching. Then, my classroom experience led me to certain readings, which led me to the research, which led to a theory. But this is not a linear process at all. The theory [. . .] was evolving as I was teaching, reading, designing and carrying out my study, and writing up and sharing my work. [. . .]
>
> So why did it take me so long to characterize my work as theory building? When I look back at this process now, I see two reasons. First, it was so chaotic [. . .] and so full of uncertainty that it seemed far removed from the elegant theories that I had read. [. . .]
>
> Second, as a graduate student, I felt unprepared to propose a *theory*. I was comfortable designing, carrying out, and reporting on a study, but I was unsure how one really goes about building theory through research. [. . .] With time, however, theory has become something I see as "doable," another stage in attempting to understand particular aspects of the world we observe and participate in. I now see that research and theory share a great deal in common, as both impose order, lending coherence to the very messy, even unruly, realities of human activity. (Tardy, 2010, pp. 123–124)

So take heart. Be patient. Keep searching. Keep building your knowledge, bit by bit.

Summary of Main Points in This Chapter

1. A concept is an idea that is more abstract than concrete empirical data. A theory is a network or model of related concepts.

2. Fear of theory is common because theoretical thinking removes us from the concrete and practical realities of a research project.

3. Whether doctoral students use formal Big T theories or less formal concepts, they need to frame their projects as a way to ensure coherence, focus, and connection to other work.

4. It is important to learn enough about theories and concepts so that discussion. of them in a doctoral project stems from genuine understanding rather than name dropping.

☞ *Suggestions for Discussion and Reflection* ☜

1. What is your understanding of the terms *theory* and *concept*?

2. How attracted or resistant are you to theoretical and conceptual thinking? Why do you think you are either attracted or resistant?

3. In your doctoral program so far, what theories or concepts have you encountered in your readings or class sessions? Which ones seem promising for helping frame a study you might do? Do you feel pressured by advisers or other professors to choose or develop theories for your doctoral project?

Chapter 7

Finding Advisers-Supervisors and Mentors

┌─ MYTH #7 ─────────────────────────────────────┐

Professors can be trusted to know more than doctoral students will ever know.

It is very easy to be intimidated by your professors, particularly if they are well-known and keep their office doors closed much of the time. But they were not born with a PhD diploma in their hands. They all suffered through the same processes you are going through now. And many of them continue to be secretly overwhelmed by all that they do not yet, and never will, know. But in their role as adviser, they are not likely to confess this to you.

└───┘

I begin this chapter with two stories of a doctoral student's search for an adviser. The first story is my own, from a long time ago (mid-1980s). The second story is more recent, from the longitudinal case study of "Mariko," one of three Japanese women

95

in U.S. university graduate programs studied by Hood (in preparation) as part of his own doctoral dissertation.

Story 1: My search for an adviser

> When I started my PhD program, I had no idea how students were selected for admission. It was much later when, as a student member of an admissions committee, I realized that students were selected by faculty in the department according to who they thought might fit their own agendas and interests. I recall being stunned as a student member at an admissions committee meeting when a well-known person in applied linguistics, with a stellar record of grades and publications, was not selected for admission to the doctoral program. Apparently no faculty member on the committee found her goals and background compatible with their own and so were not willing to take her on as an advisee.
>
> In my own case, I was chosen by Robert Politzer, a second language specialist in bilingualism, who I found out later had 30 advisees. Normal is perhaps five. After a pre-admission interview with him, I never saw him again. He had a complete breakdown, and even though he did not pass away until 1998, he was not able to continue his work. His advisees were distributed among other faculty, temporarily, until all of us could find someone else. This is how I got to know Shirley Brice Heath, a coincidence for which I was grateful, but it was clear early on that she could not take me on permanently. I took a sociology class with another well-known person in the department and thought she might fit the bill. But by the end of the quarter, I knew it was a bad choice: She was demanding, prescriptive, and devoted to counting things that I thought could not and should not be counted. I recall her saying one day in class, in an imperious tone, "If I can describe it, I can

count it." I then began working on some ideas involving what I called "forms of representation" in scholarly work (signs, symbols, terminology in scholarly discourse), and went to talk to another very well-known recent addition to the department, a cognitive psychologist. After explaining what I was thinking of doing, he leaned back in his chair and said that he would take me on only if I gave up what I was doing and followed what he told me to do. Instant clash of style, and I never went back. (I have a "don't-tell-me-what-to-do" type of personality, for better or worse.)

When I discovered the joys of more qualitatively oriented reading and writing research in courses with a husband-wife team, I felt more at home, and pursued connections with both of them throughout the rest of my dissertation journey. To this day, I wonder what would have happened if I had not been agentive in finding an adviser and had simply followed a professor's program and methods of research. I think I would have been quite miserable.

Story 2: Mariko's search for an adviser

Mariko had no adviser for the first three terms. When he [the adviser] finally returned from sabbatical, he offered very little advice. This was perhaps his style (hands off, let them figure it out), but it was absolutely the wrong style for Mariko, who really needed someone to be prescriptive with her. She had incredible anxiety about choosing a dissertation topic, which she had to do before forming a committee to write her prelim test. Mariko had no idea how to narrow down a topic, and Nelson was not going to help her. She was months behind on this when I last saw her (in February, 2011). This problem was made worse by the very few choices she had for committee members—the one she was most interested in working with

was. . .ON SABBATICAL! Mariko failed her prelims and
that was it. I need to ask some follow-up questions about
this, how she attributes this failure. I'm sure she will blame
herself, and she would be partly correct. But I think that
with better guidance she would have made it. (Hood, email
communication, July 13, 2013)

These introductory stories highlight a question of utmost
concern for doctoral students from the time they begin their
program: Who will their adviser be and will he or she be compatible, helpful, and around for the long term? In U.S. universities, the choice of adviser becomes crucial as students finish up
course work, begin to design a project, and prepare to write a
dissertation proposal. In U.K. systems, the adviser (or supervisor
in U.K. terminology) is in students' lives from day one and is one
of the main sources of students' learning and progress. A good
match of topics and personalities as well as productive "advising
behaviors" by faculty and continuity over time seem crucial (Ives
& Rowley, 2005; Paltridge & Woodrow, 2012; Zhao, Golde, &
McCormick, 2007), but there is no guarantee of such a match.
Finding and sustaining productive relationships in doctoral work
turns out to be quite challenging, regardless of discipline or loca-
tion of the university.

The issue of good advising is addressed extensively in educational literature in U.K. systems, perhaps because the supervisor is such a central figure in graduate students' lives throughout
the entire doctoral process. Problems are common, and questions about whether doctoral supervisors need training, so they
won't simply repeat poor advising techniques they might have
been subject to themselves, have been raised (Halse & Malfroy,
2010; Lee, 2007, 2008; Li & Seale, 2007). In all settings, however,
the dilemma for advisers-supervisors is how involved or directive
to be in students work. Tensions and contrasts in style between
dominance and neglect are infamous (Delamont, Parry, & Atkin-

son, 1998), and conflicts and paradoxical demands often characterize the adviser-student relationship (Vilkinas, 2008). Styles of advising differ as well according to whether students' projects are closely connected with the research an adviser is doing or are conducted independently (Franke & Arvidsson, 2011). Clearly an adviser has much more at stake in students' projects and progress if the research is closely tied with his or her own work and is therefore likely to pay fairly close attention to students on his or her team. Students who design independent doctoral dissertations, in contrast, must find advisers who have both interest in and at least some knowledge of the students' areas of interest. In this latter case, students need to find ways to work with their advisers as "legitimate peripheral participants" in developing research skills (Hasrati, 2005) or risk suffering from neglect.

Advisers-supervisors are not the same as mentors. All doctoral students have some kind of adviser (whether the relationship is a successful one or not) but not all have mentors. Mentors provide a kind of emotional support that is not characteristic of typical adviser-advisee relationships (Casanave & Li, 2012; Lee, 2007). I'll write more about mentors in the last section of this chapter. Suffice it to say for now that real mentors are rare, that most of us pine for one, and that most of us manage to survive without one.

Of special concern to scholars in English-medium graduate education throughout the world are the experiences of nonnative users of English and their relationships with their advisers (Belcher, 1994; Cadman, 2000; Casanave, 2010b; Dong, 1998; Fujioka, 2008; Hood (in preparation); Kim, 2007; Ohashi, Ohashi, & Paltridge, 2008). International students need first to understand what the expected roles of advisers and doctoral students are, and then to be strategic and agentive in their relationships with advisers to prevent being neglected. In a study of the reflective web postings of 27 master's and doctoral students from different countries who were writing theses and dissertations at an Australian university, Paltridge and Woodrow (2012, p. 100) learned that "concerns with supervisor relations . . . emerged as an issue of importance for the students," often reflecting "a mismatch in student and supervisor perceptions of what their respective roles are." Some of my experiences at an American university in Japan confirm their findings: I've had a few cases in which a Japanese advisee expected me to give "assignments" every step of the way. While I was waiting for a student to contact me and send me something, the student was waiting to be assigned something.

Finally, we can ask whether gender influences the adviser-student relationship. Zhao, Golde, and McCormick (2008) say yes—that women in their study were more dissatisfied with their relationships with their advisers than were men, even though both were likely to feel exploited by them in certain disciplines, particularly in the sciences.

In the remainder of this chapter, I deal with some of these issues in more detail. I discuss them mainly from the point of view of doctoral students. The issues concern understanding an adviser's roles in a university, finding appropriate advisers, changing and managing advisers, and the elusiveness of real mentors.

☞ Putting an Adviser's Role in Perspective

As disappointing as this news might be to many students, doctoral advisers do not consider you to be the center of their professional lives. Advising is one university duty among many, and in some cases, a duty that they take on reluctantly. Depending on the university and the status of your adviser, he or she might also be advising other students, teaching, doing research that he or she finds far more engaging than your project, serving on committees, writing grants, performing some kind of community service, writing books and articles, and for the lucky or determined ones, enjoying some kind of personal life. You deserve attention from your adviser, but it might be a good idea to learn early on, as part of your search (assuming you have some choice), what your prospective adviser's life is like beyond the time you hope is spent with you. And remember, advisers who do not yet have tenure will be consumed with the activities required to help them keep their own jobs. Advising might not be high on the list. That said, there are many professors, regardless of status, who *like* the activity of advising—they find the first-hand, in-person contact with novice scholars both interesting and stimulating and the possibilities of learning from them and influencing them quite appealing.

☞ Searching with an Open Mind from the Beginning

It is possible that, like many first-year doctoral students, you were assigned an adviser when you entered your program. This professor might have been one who selected you for admission, thinking that your interests and goals matched his or hers well. The allocation might also have been an administrative one of dividing up students among the available pool of advisers. Without your active involvement, you may or may not have been assigned the right person to see you through the program. You will know quite quickly, once you have taken some classes with this person and met with him or her one or more times. You will click with the person, or find yourself feeling unsure or neutral, or be genuinely turned off.

If the person that you have been assigned to does not seem compatible, or if the person just does not seem to have time for or interest in you, then you can look around for someone else, possibly even someone not directly part of your program. As I described at the beginning of this chapter, I faced that challenge in my own doctoral program because my initially assigned adviser left the program because of illness. My search was complicated by the fact that I started my doctoral program as someone interested in applied linguistics. But there were no tenured applied linguists in the program since the demise of my initial adviser. I then paid attention to the characteristics of all the professors I had classes with for the first couple of years, trying to figure out if they would make suitable advisers, even though I was not sure what I wanted my dissertation research to be about. What jumped out at me was the subject matter the professors taught, the readings they assigned, the research methods they seemed to be most comfortable with, and their personalities (including presence or absence of a sense of humor). In all cases I asked whether my interest was sparked by this person and his or her research areas and methods.

I was thus forced to keep an open mind from the beginning in my search for an adviser, because there was no one in the department who was an expert in what I thought I wanted to study. My horizons broadened as a result, and I discovered that "reading," "writing," and "linguistics and language acquisition" didn't need to restrict me to a focus on second language issues. I began to see that scholars in first language literacy and composition and in theoretical linguistics and child language acquisition could help me understand some of the miracles of language. Ultimately, it was from professors in those fields that I found advisers for my major and minor specializations. It took a while, but it was worth the search and the wait.

Finding the right person to work with, particularly as you get closer to planning and carrying out a dissertation project, might make the difference between success and failure. You need to be pro-active in your search.

☞ Assessing an Adviser's Knowledge, Interests, Commitment, and Expectations

It is incumbent upon doctoral students early in their program to do some homework about their advisers or potential advisers. Remember: They don't know everything, can't do everything, and are themselves continuing to learn, even if they are authorities in their fields. Some questions to ask about your potential advisers are: What do you know about this professor? What is this professor's history of publications and research projects? Does he or she share references with students and guide them to useful resources? Will you be taking, or have you taken, courses with this person? What seem to be his or her main areas of interest and favorite research methods? What is the professor's reputation in the department among other students? In your initial encounters with this adviser, what chemistry do you have with this person? What are this person's relationships like with other professors that you might be working with? And does it look like the professor will be around for the duration of your program?

One of the most important initial meetings you have with a potential adviser concerns what expectations you have of each other in the adviser-advisee relationship (Paltridge & Woodrow, 2012). How often does each of you expect to meet, and for what purposes? Some advisers want to see you only if you have submitted a piece of writing to them; they see their job as providing critique and feedback on writing, assuming that they have not lost your work in the bowels of a cluttered office or an unorganized computer file, and that they have read it carefully and remember what you have written (I speak from experience). They might or might not give their advisees tasks and deadlines; advisees might expect such tasks and deadlines and be disappointed if they don't get detailed instructions about what to do. In my case, I wished to work more at my own pace but wanted access to and guidance and encouragement from advisers. Some advisers are willing to talk with advisees at the early planning stages of a dissertation project, but others expect to meet infrequently over concrete pieces of writing. Ultimately students and advisers need to agree on how directive and structured the relationship will be, which is not always an easy decision (Delamont, Parry, & Atkinson, 1998). In general, advisers expect doctoral students to develop enough independence and autonomy so that "hand-holding" is not needed, but beyond that, the relationships are quite diverse, from excessive control at one end to excessive laissez-faire at the other.

A main point of asking yourself such questions is to recognize the responsibilities you have in the adviser-advisee relationship and the agency you have in making choices of who your main adviser is. If the match is not comfortable, you can consider changing.

⌒ Changing Advisers, If Necessary

Although it might not be possible in all university systems, it is generally possible for students to change advisers if the relationship is not working well. Reasons for problems are various. A common one is neglect (see the case of Mariko in Story 2 at the beginning of this chapter). Some advisers simply don't have or make time to consult often enough with advisees. In a doctoral program, once a semester is not enough. Story 2, of Mariko, tells an extreme case of neglect; as a Japanese graduate student, she traveled to the United States for doctoral work and found that the adviser had left on a sabbatical shortly after the student arrived without arranging for a replacement adviser for her. She was left on her own to find someone new, a search that was never resolved satisfactorily (Hood, in preparation). Other cases involve clashes of interests or beliefs about what constitutes an appropriate topic and research method in the doctoral student's work. If an adviser dismisses a student's interests or commitment to a particular research approach, the relationship is not likely to be productive. The question to be asked is, what can advisers do to help students learn things that are compatible with students' interests and strengths as well as the adviser's own interests? It is easy to sense when a professor has little interest in or patience with students' work—this is a sign for students to make some kind of change.

Another kind of mismatch arises from clashes of personality and style. True conflicts are rare, I think (but see Sternberg, 1981), but need to be acknowledged. Students will know quickly whether they feel comfortable around their adviser(s) and their working styles or if the chemistry just won't work. A tight stomach and a sense of dread before a meeting are signs of danger. All this being said, relationships between advisers and students take time to evolve, as does any close and important relationship. But students need to keep their eyes open to signs of problems.

In the story that follows, Mayumi Fujioka (2008) tells of the difficult dilemma she faced in her doctoral program at a midwestern U.S. university—that of needing to change advisers. As a female international student from Japan, she had little idea at first that students who were having problems with their current adviser could take agentive steps to make changes. From one perspective, this would involve challenging the hierarchy of authority in her department. She did know, however, that she had to select an adviser and committee members herself, which she did at her proposal stage. The professors' names are pseudonyms; the story is quoted directly.

Story 3: Mayumi Fujioka and her change of adviser

> After asking Dr. Anderson to be my main advisor, I started working with her on my dissertation proposal. As I proceeded with my proposal, however, I began to feel that my style of work and hers did not match; I felt that I was not getting enough dialogical, face-to-face interactions with her, given that she seemed to prefer a rather hierarchical and impersonal style of communication through email. [. . .] In addition, I began to feel that she was more eager to make me complete my dissertation as soon as possible than I was [. . .] Although I understood that she was trying to help me, I began to feel that she was almost sending a message that she did not care about the quality of my study as long as I could finish it within the proposed timeline. [. . .] At the same time, I started seriously doubting if the topic I was proposing was the topic

that I would really like to explore. Even so, I kept writing my proposal as the deadline that Dr. Anderson and I had agreed on was approaching.

A month after I started working with Dr. Anderson, I had almost completed a draft of my dissertation proposal. At that point, I had to choose a third member on my dissertation committee, and I decided to ask Dr. Brown. [. . .] The main reason I asked her to be on my committee was that among doctoral students, she was recognized as being the best person to ask for help with a dissertation . . . . [. . .] I wrote a two-page prospectus based on my dissertation proposal, submitted it to Dr. Brown, and made an appointment with her, eager to hear from her that my topic was acceptable.

However, the response I received from Dr. Brown was contrary to my expectations. Having read my prospectus, she told me that I should rethink my topic and methodology as well. [. . .]

On the following day, I went to see Dr. Anderson, reporting to her about what Dr. Brown had told me. In fact, I even do not quite remember the details of the conversation that Dr. Anderson and I had at that meeting. The only thing I remember was that I did not think I received help from her. [. . .] Another thing I remember was that I felt devastated when I left Dr. Anderson's office. . . .

[After deciding to change my topic], I went to talk with Dr. Brown, who was surprised at my quick decision to change the topic but kindly agreed to be my main advisor. [. . .] [T]he task of talking to the two professors, Dr. Anderson in particular, was very difficult. I thought that I was in danger of hurting and offending her. Yet, I decided to take the risk mainly because I now knew what I wanted to study and knew this was going to be MY dissertation, not anyone else's. Fortunately, I received understanding and even encouragement from both professors for my topic change. (Fujioka, 2008, pp. 64–65)

☞ Managing Your Advisers

Once you have found an adviser to work with, it is up to you to manage the interactions and negotiations, especially if you feel you are being ignored or not guided in productive ways. Easier said than done, of course. It is common to feel intimidated and vulnerable in interactions with a professor who seems to know everything and to hold so much power over you. And in some educational systems, students simply do not take any lead at all in managing these interactions; students see their role as one of recipient and listener, not active agent or balanced negotiator. Even less common is for students to see themselves as possible contributors to a professor's own knowledge. (But believe it or not, one valuable source of professors' knowledge comes from their students.) It is difficult to change both beliefs and practices about this role, so it's a good topic for discussion among classmates.

Another reason that such interactions can be difficult is that some professors find advising, particularly at the labor-intensive dissertation planning and writing stages, to be one of their least favorite academic responsibilities. Advising takes a great deal of time away from their own work (unless their advisees are part of their research team), it requires being interested in someone else's work besides their own, and it requires a long-term commitment to people they might not be culturally or personally comfortable with. Stories abound, for example, of mismatches between Western scholars and non-Western advisees who hold different expectations about what each is supposed to be doing in the advising relationship. Not only might advisers be overly busy, but getting what you want from an adviser who is neglectful, forgetful, abusive, overly perfectionist, or otherwise unhelpful can also be tricky: How can students deal with professors in ways that are firm but not rude or demanding? How can they be organized and clear about what they want from a professor without coming across as excessively dependent or unprepared for doctoral research? How can they insist on being treated with respect rather than having their work or their plans dismissed by means of demeaning critiques? And importantly, how can students learn to take advantage of the informal interactions between them and advisers, which might turn out to be more important for their learning than formal meetings (Hasrati, 2005)?

It can be difficult for both native English and nonnative English speakers to manage such negotiations in successful ways. However, most faculty in a program have reputations for being easy or difficult to get along with, and classmates can often provide hints and suggestions for how to approach a particular professor for purposes of negotiating the relationship. The point is: Don't sit back and wait for an adviser to come to you. Take action, and, if necessary, in the company of friends to give you courage.

☞ The Rarity of Real Mentors

As I mentioned in the introduction to this chapter, real mentors are a rarity in academia, and certainly not an expected element in the structure and function of a department. Every doctoral program needs to match advisers with students, but there is no universal requirement for the department to provide students with mentors. I was lucky in my program to have some helpful and cordial advising relationships, but I am not sure that I would use the term *mentor* to describe the faculty who assisted me.

Advisers and mentors play different roles. In the U.S. context, advisers, according to Creighton, Creighton, and Parks (2010), should be assigned when students enter a doctoral program and help them take care of administrative matters connected with pursuing the doctoral degree: here is what you need to do to get through the doctoral program and to finish a dissertation. Mentors, on the other hand, are best connected with students a bit later and serve as role models and partners in learning. Ideally, "The mentor provides the student with an environment of reciprocity, where the faculty member benefits professionally as much from the relationship as does the student" (Creighton, Creighton, & Parks, 2010, p. 42). I am not sure the extent to which professors in doctoral programs see themselves as co-learners with their students or, in contrast, as authoritative sources of topic knowledge and research methods whose job it is to provide advice and direction to students. As I look back to my own doctoral years, I don't know if the main faculty who helped me at various stages of my dissertation work also learned anything from me. I know that I have learned a great deal from my own doctoral students, but I fear I have not let them know often enough how much they have taught me.

Mentors have another role, too. They provide emotional support, as well as other kinds of support, that can help mentees through difficult times. The emotional and intellectual support is ideally reciprocal in doctoral programs and later in collaborations between novice and established scholars (Casanave & Li, 2012). In doctoral programs, however, some advisers might find the idea of emotional support inappropriate and beyond the call of duty, even though mentees can benefit greatly. Lee (2007) asserted that the emotional bond is the main strength of the mentor-mentee relationship because it can help students develop confidence and agency:

> The primary mentor can provide a more profound experience and some supervisors will feel that this goes beyond what they are expected to do. When an emotional bond is developed the mentee is deemed to have a primary mentor. The strength of the primary mentor is that they provide acceptance and confirmation that the mentee is worthwhile and this leads to personal empowerment. (Lee, 2007, p. 686)

I agree. But this claim could be seen as a bit paradoxical—if mentors provide substantial intellectual and emotional support to doctoral students, might not such a relationship develop into one of dependency on the part of students rather than empowerment? I suppose this is possible, but I think it is more likely that students are encouraged by such a relationship to find their way through the long years of doctoral study without becoming discouraged and despondent. Sometimes a personal and emotional connection with a mentor is needed to convince students that they can succeed, even when things look quite bleak. In my own case as dissertation adviser (mentor??) of numerous mid-career, middle-aged teachers who have health problems, family responsibilities, and fatigue from excessive workloads at their schools, the most helpful thing I can do sometimes is to convince them of my sincere belief in them and their dissertation projects and to be a good listener.

Most mentor-mentee relationships are not so fraught with problems, however. Rather, they are productive, long-term relationships that are likely to endure beyond the doctoral program. Steve Simpson's mentoring relationship with Paul Kei Matsuda was one of those productive long-term relationships (Simpson & Matsuda, 2008). As Steve told it, he was at first intimidated by working with someone like Paul, who was one of the main reasons Steve applied to the university where Paul was working. However, Paul involved him and other advisees in a "series of tasks designed to move his mentees toward increased participation in the field" (p. 95). The tasks included proofreading professional publications and learning about the publication process, assisting with research tasks such as transcribing conversational data, and participating in activities in their field's main conference on first and second language writing. This mentoring relationship lasted for more than five years and served as acculturation into the profession, well beyond the support that Steve also received on his dissertation work. As Steve and Paul conclude:

> The mentor and mentee [. . .] need to build a strong working relationship in which their needs and concerns can be expressed freely so that the mentor is aware of the mentee's interest, development, and strengths and weaknesses. The relationship also needs to be healthy and sustainable. That is, both parties need to benefit mutually from the experience— and feel that they do. (Simpson & Matsuda, 2008, p. 101)

If by the end of this chapter you still are hesitant to take a proactive stance in seeking and managing relations with an adviser and still are intimidated by fame or authority, go back to the myth that I tried to dispel at the beginning of the chapter: Your own professors have chosen the university life because they themselves have so much yet to learn. You can help them in their knowledge journey, as they will help you. As one of the supervisors in Hasrati's (2005) study of Iranian doctoral students in the U.K. said:

> In three years time, when we get to the end of it, the student-supervisor relationship is changed completely. . . . [then] it is the student who knows 95% of it and the supervisor who knows 5%. So the roles are reversed. (Hasrati, 2005, p. 564)

On the other hand, if it seems impossible to find any resources at all for advising or mentoring in your department, it might be time to consider transferring to another department or university. Try to find this out early in your doctoral program.

Summary of Main Points in This Chapter

1. Doctoral students in U.S.- and U.K.-style programs need to be proactive in seeking, managing, and, if needed, changing advisers.

2. It is essential for students and advisers to meet early in their relationship and lay out clearly what they expect from each other. Some conflicting expectations might result from cultural or personality differences, or different interests and preferred research methods.

3. Advisers and mentors have different roles. Every doctoral student has an adviser, but real mentors are quite rare. Mentors provide students with emotional support and opportunities to participate in professional activities.

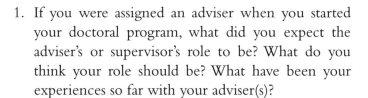

Suggestions for Discussion and Reflection

1. If you were assigned an adviser when you started your doctoral program, what did you expect the adviser's or supervisor's role to be? What do you think your role should be? What have been your experiences so far with your adviser(s)?

2. If you are not satisfied with your relationship with your adviser, what steps might you take to improve things? What advice do you get from other students in your program about working and negotiating with particular advisers?

3. Have you ever had a real mentor? How do you characterize the qualities of a real mentor? In a reciprocal relationship with a mentor, what do you think you can offer him or her?

Chapter 8

Seeking Supportive People

The main reason to seek and establish firm ties with supportive people before you start to write your dissertation is that
once you are done with course work (if you are in a program that
requires course work), everyone in the department scatters and
you are left isolated, particularly if you are not living on or near
your university campus. If you are living far from home, this stage

of doctoral work can be doubly isolating. But even if you are at home with a family that provides security and emotional comfort, the support of colleagues and friends who have had similar experiences in graduate school is essential. As isolating as doctoral work can be—as can researching and writing for publication as part of an academic career later—successful doctoral students and career academics maintain ties with others for intellectual and emotional support.

I wish I knew how to make such connections with supportive people work better than they often do, but I don't know how to ensure that they happen. People who are geographically scattered as well as involved in full- or part-time work, as often happens before the doctoral degree is in hand, struggle to maintain connections with others. Busy schedules, lack of energy, lack of easy access in person, reluctance to impose on others' time through frequent telephone or skype calls or lengthy emails, and a sometimes obsessive focus on students' own projects all work against maintaining contact with supportive people. Families and partners are supportive in their own ways, but as I will discuss further, might not fully understand what doctoral students are going through, be able to discuss research- or writing-oriented issues with them, or comprehend why it takes so long to complete a dissertation. Many of my own classmates, and I too, were the first in their families to pursue a doctoral degree. Our families did not know what was involved and they didn't fully understand when we tried to explain.

The kinds of support you get from colleagues, friends, and family differ from the support you get from even the best of advisers. An adviser has a job to do, which is to help you complete a large research project and write it up as a highly constrained and conventionalized document that follows the rules of a particular university. When advisers do their jobs well, students feel supported intellectually and emotionally, and connected to their departments. However, this job tends to be one way; students rarely learn much about what their advisers are going through or have opportunities to support them intellectually or emotionally. I cannot recall a single instance in my career when an adviser or other faculty member called a student in to her office to ask for help or advice of any kind, or even just to have a chat. If chats happen, it is often because circumstances bring professors and students together at the same social gathering, not because professors reach out to students.

Other kinds of supportive people fill in the inevitable gaps in the unbalanced faculty-student relationship. Supportive people such as classmates and friends inside and outside a department can think and learn along with each other; provide reality checks when students' language and thinking seem to have vaulted into outer space; offer emotional support by commiserating in hard times and celebrating even the smallest of successes; encourage each other to maintain a healthy and active lifestyle when it seems impossible for dissertation writers to tear themselves away from the computer; and stimulate reciprocal support, from one to the other, in acts of generosity that will help each other keep going on their own projects. Not only do connections with others feed into a dissertation project (through shared discussions, readings, classes), but connections can help doctoral students de-center now and then to see outside their own preoccupations. If students are isolated, they cannot easily do this.

As I discussed in Chapter 1, there is some evidence that isolation is one of main causes of attrition in doctoral programs, particularly at the departmental level: "Students who leave their doctoral program are likely to be unconnected to the academic and social life of the department" (Golde, 2000, p. 202). In other words, support from outside the department might not be enough. Colleagues and friends inside the department are needed as well. Of course, people do manage to survive more or less on their own, but perhaps with much more suffering than they need to endure.

I end this introduction with a story of Natsuko Kuwahara (2008), who recounted the stress of her first year in her doctoral program and her strategies for reaching out. She had gotten her MA degree in the United States but had returned to Japan to teach English for several years before deciding to apply for a doctoral program in a prestigious U.S. school of education. As is the case for many new doctoral students, her first year was filled with anxiety and self-doubt and "a deep sense of guilt that I wasn't meeting the expectations of my professors, of my peers, and of all the people who had worked so hard to give me the opportunity to go to graduate school in the U.S." (p. 186). "I was certainly thrilled with being a student again," she continued, "but the change from being a native speaker in Japan to a non-native speaker in the U.S. was harder than expected" (p. 189). Isolation characterized the start of her first year, prompting her to seek academic and emotional support. The following is quoted directly from a book chapter she wrote.

Story 1: Natsuko's strategic search for support

During my first semester, I took part in two study groups.
. . . Each group provided distinct learning experiences and facilitated my socialization in different ways.

The peer group was formed with two other students from my cohort who were taking the same classes I was. Each week, we met to discuss articles assigned in these classes. [. . .]

I also joined another study group, which included a faculty member and five students from her class. [. . .] [T]hrough closer personal contact with a professor, I was able to see my professors as real people and started to feel more comfortable when talking to them. [. . .]

When building a support network, it is important to remember that even the best academics require support from non-academic sources. [. . .] Important resources include the Financial Aid Office, Doctoral Program administrators, the Career Development Office, Student Affairs, and the International Students Office. [...]

Support from native speakers was influential in assisting my academic progress. . . . However, I also needed emotional support from people who had either experienced or were experiencing similar struggles. In this, I was lucky to be around other international advanced doctoral students and other Japanese students and researchers. While international advanced doctoral students allowed me to see what successful non-native doctoral students look like in my own field, the Japanese academic community provided a place to feel at home and take comfort in my abilities without having to face a communication barrier. [. . .] (Kuwahara, 2008, pp. 192–194)

What characterized Natusko's strategies in her first year was that she reached out, proactively, beyond the immediate circle of an adviser and a few professors. Because she was living far from her home in Japan, she could not depend on immediate family members for support; she found a way to connect with other Japanese students and researchers, among other resource people, instead. In the remainder of this chapter, I discuss some of these kinds of connections that can help students on their journey—connections with cohort and study group members, individual classmates, departments, and friends and family. I end with another short story from Natsuko.

⌒ Cohorts and Study Groups

Some doctoral programs admit students in cohorts that they hope will form bonds for the duration of their programs. In programs that require course work, including core courses that all students must take, students go through the same learning experiences and challenges together and so naturally establish bonds with one or more classmates. The first-year doctoral program in sociology that I observed for my own dissertation project worked like this. The students were even given office carrels in the same large room, the department's spatial strategy for ensuring maximum contact among students during their three years of course work. They attended core classes together and saw each other daily in the common office space.

However, physical co-presence does not ensure that students will form supportive bonds at the pre-dissertation stage. Friendships are based on trust and chemistry, not just association. The point is for students to place a high priority on establishing bonds with even one or two other people who look like they can be trusted to provide intellectual and emotional support over time. In the program I observed for my dissertation project, as well as in my own department, these bonds sometimes formed outside the cohort, often with students a year or two ahead, ones who knew the ropes and knew how to play the game (Casanave, 2002). In the sociology department where I did my research, a Chinese woman found that there were three other students from mainland China in the department, all ahead of her at different stages of the doctoral program. She relied heavily on them for help and emotional support during the first several years. Two of my own main supports were classmates who were one year ahead of me.

Study groups are particularly useful for helping doctoral students survive difficult courses that they are all taking together. They are relatively easy to establish during the course work stage because people tend to be physically present and able to meet in person, but almost impossible to continue once students have finished course work and scattered to work on their own projects. If several people in a study group live within commuting distance of each other, then it is possible to make a strong commitment to meet regularly on or off campus even after course work is completed. Usually one person needs to take charge of organizing study group meetings—left on our own, most of us will watch the time fly by without making efforts to meet. It is therefore important for students to make one or more strong connections early in a doctoral program—ones that might last into the dissertation writing stage.

Still, by the time proposals need to be written and data collected, I think it is common for students to fold in on themselves and become preoccupied to the point of obsessiveness with their own projects. Hermitish behavior abounds. At the actual writing stage, it is possible for dissertation writers to lose friends, be threatened with divorce, and to slack off job responsibilities if they are working—such is the pull of the dissertation writing process and the associated fears and anxieties. The other response to this pressure is that the dissertation is neglected for months at a time, possibly leading students to eventually drop out. Strong bonds with cohort members and classmates, formed early, help students stand a chance of surviving the hermit stage later. After all, everyone in the group is going through the same thing; no one is really alone in their struggles.

⌒ Individual Classmates

It may be that one or more individual classmates become a lifeline for you. The advantage of a close and supportive connection to a couple of people in your program is that they know what you are experiencing. Understanding and support are mutual, and long and complicated background stories, once learned about each other, do not need to be repeated in order to explain a problem or confusion. Mutual trust is essential in such departmental relationships because the relationship is likely to involve shared knowledge and experiences, emotions, gossip, confidences and secrets, and common knowledge of the same faculty and classmates. Potentially dangerous territory! But imagine the relief of having someone around whom you do not have to pretend to be strong and smart all the time, with whom you can share your sense of humor, and with whom you can share strategies for dealing with difficult people and situations. It takes time to build such trusting relationships, but they can enrich the doctoral experience immeasurably and help you through difficult times.

☞ Staying Connected to the Department

As I have mentioned elsewhere, one of the main causes of attrition in doctoral programs is students' lack of connection with their departments. A big part of this connection is good relations with advisers (see Chapter 7) as well as with classmates. But it is a mistake for students to rely on advisers or key faculty as their sole source of advice and of intellectual and emotional support. Regular contact with an adviser or other faculty member is a goal for students to strive for but not to depend on. Advisers are famous for neglecting doctoral students or being unnecessarily critical (Sternberg, 1981). Therefore, another essential connection revolves around other people such as those discussed in the previous sections. Additionally, as explained by Kuwahara (2008) in Story 1, non-departmental staff people can provide essential support. I would add librarians to her list. Such staff people are generally willing to help with problems or questions, and in my experience often have time for a smile and brief chat, unlike many busy professors. Also, if such staff people know students personally, they are especially willing to help.

An equally important connection to the department, apart from that with an adviser and classmates, is to department events that might be taking place periodically. It is at such events that students can meet up with others and participate in discussions, presentations, and lectures. This means that students who are living off campus need to check email or website announcements regularly to stay abreast of what might be going on. Have any interesting speakers been invited to departmental or university-wide events? Are there any gatherings of students in the program that offer a forum for them to present their evolving work in informal presentations? If not, can students organize such forums on their own? What social events, if any, does the department host? The point is to know what events take place and make efforts to attend some of them as a way to stay connected.

☞ Friends and Family

Friends and family who are outside your department and who have no connection with your dissertation project can provide valuable respite from excessive focus on dissertation work. They can remind you that the world continues to function around you and that it awaits you when your dissertation is completed. They can offer you perspective on your life and work and help pull you out of any mires you might find yourself in. They are your evidence that more exists in your world than your doctoral dissertation. The dissertation work is temporary; your relationships are permanent. Good friendships and relationships with beloved partners and family members need to be protected, and that means finding a way to make even a modicum of time for them.

However, it might not mean involving them deeply in your dissertation project. By the time students reach the dissertation proposal and later the writing stage, they have learned the "second language" of their disciplines (sociology as a second language, applied linguistics as a second language, psychology as a second language. . .). This "new" language is a second language for both native and nonnative speakers of English—everyone learns the terminology together and that terminology begins to bring concepts and ideas into existence that might not have been visible before and that cannot easily be explained in everyday language. I recall the sadness with which one of my case study participants, "Virginia," reported to me in the second year of her sociology program that she could no longer explain to her mother what she was doing (Casanave, 1992). This was her clue that it was time for her to leave the doctoral program. I had a similar experience with my parents and sister once I was at the proposal stage. I was not able to talk with them about my dissertation project in ways they could understand.

All the more reason to de-center now and then, and focus (even if briefly) on the handful of precious loved ones in your life.

To conclude this short chapter on an upbeat note, let me quote another part of Natsuko Kuwahara's story of her first year struggles to find support networks.

Story 2: Natsuko's first year successes

> By the end of the first year, I started to feel more comfortable with my role as a doctoral student. I found myself taking the initiative more often, conducting an independent study, choosing my adviser, and applying for grants and fellowships, all of which would have seemed impossible at the start of my first year. I also became more involved in my own work and the supporting network I was establishing inside and outside of school. Taking initiative and becoming more involved required constant investment but were crucial during my first year.... [...]
>
> Graduate school is often described as a lonely journey. Getting through graduate school, however, cannot be accomplished by oneself, especially in the case of non-native speakers. Since the first year in [a] doctoral program is often critical for setting the stage for the rest of the graduate school experience, finding supportive mentors and creating supportive networks beyond the classroom are keys to overcoming non-native and foreigner status. (Kuwahara, 2008, pp. 198–199)

I think one does not have to be a nonnative English user to benefit from supportive mentors and networks of colleagues and friends. Everyone benefits.

To return to the myth of independence and autonomy: Pure independence and autonomy do not exist. Everyone in academic life relies on connections with others to get work done, to solve problems, and to survive intellectually and emotionally. But no one is likely to hold your hand and lead you through your program. It will be up to you to reach out and forge the connections that will help you survive. Once course work is done, connections might be less frequent, primarily electronic, and difficult to maintain, but they should not be abandoned.

Summary of Main Points in This Chapter

1. Establishing strong ties with people inside and outside the department can help doctoral students avoid the isolation that often comes later during the dissertation writing stage.

2. Important supportive connections within a department are those that students make with cohort members, study groups, individual classmates, and department and administrative staff. It is a mistake to rely on professors and advisers for all the support that is needed.

3. Departmental events serve to bring doctoral students together, even if infrequently.

4. Friends, partners, and family are wonderful, but sometimes distant, sources of support for doctoral students. They provide escape from the pressure of the academic work but might not be able to understand enough about the language, concepts, and activities of doctoral research to be good conversation partners.

5. Students need to be active agents in forging their own connections with supportive people.

⌒ *Suggestions for Discussion and Reflection* ⌒

1. At your current stage in your doctoral program, what kinds of connections do you have with cohort members, study group members, and individual classmates? In what ways do these groups and people support you?

2. If you feel the need to establish more connections inside your department, what steps might you take to do this?

3. What kinds of departmental events are available to you? Which events suit your need to stay connected to your department, contribute to your learning, and fulfill social needs?

4. To what extent are you able to share with family and friends outside the school setting some of the ideas, issues, and problems associated with doctoral work? In what ways are family and friends helpful and not so helpful in supporting your doctoral journey?

5. What is your understanding of the goals of independence and autonomy in doctoral work?

Chapter 9

Topic and Project Development and Refinement

If you have actually read through all the previous chapters in this small book before arriving at this last one and if you have not been scared off by some of the realities described herein, you are probably now really ready to forge ahead. This means committing to completing the doctoral program and beginning at this point to think about writing and defending a dissertation proposal, if you haven't already done that. However, if you skipped

125

the earlier chapter (Chapter 4) on topic development, go back and skim that now. This chapter builds on those initial ideas on topics. To repeat an important message from that chapter, the goal for your dissertation is to develop a topic that is lasting—one that will hold your interest, be substantial enough for a major research project, and be supported by an adviser. Neither the topic nor the methods nor the dissertation need to be perfect; they just need to be good and, above all, meaningful for you. As you refine your topic, the entire design for your project will fall into place.

You might want to look to other books and other kinds of human and textual mentors for guidance as you refine your topic, decide on your methods, and find your way into and through the early stages of the actual research project (e.g., Becker, 1986, 1998; Creswell, 2014; Kilbourn, 2006; Krathwohl & Smith, 2005; Locke, Spirduso, & Silverman, 1999; Maxwell, 2005, 2012, 2013). However, I hope that by the time you finish reading and reflecting on this chapter you will be ready to jump into the proposal stage, or to continue the work that you have already started.

In my own experience and that of numerous colleagues and doctoral students I know, the topic refinement and proposal stages are actually more difficult and intimidating than the rest of the dissertation work that follows. This is probably not only because the commitment to a proposal for a major research project is a scary moment, but also because the process leading up to it can continue to be changeable and uncertain and so can feel quite chaotic. The dissertation proposal journey has been colorfully described as "a territory marked by sweaty inclines, serene plateaus, and precipitous drops" (Kilbourn, 2006, p. 529; see also Li & Flowerdew, 2008, for the experiences of a doctoral student and her supervisor going through the confusing stage of topic and methods refinement). Happily, once you are past the proposal stage, things are likely to fall into place, and tenacity in following your plan (and we hope a supportive adviser) will get you through the long months (years?) of data collection, analysis, and writing. To reiterate a central message of this book, the hardest part of the doctoral dissertation process probably happens before the dissertation writing begins.

So in this final chapter, I return to the problems of topic development and refinement. I won't provide a checklist or a list of prescriptions because each doctoral student needs to develop the details in conjunction with guidance from and interaction with people and preferences in his or her own department. But I will reiterate a point I made in Chapter 4, that how-to books are generally not very helpful in this regard. Sections on topic choice tend to be short if they exist at all and to start after novice researchers have already identified more or less what they want to do and are ready to begin writing. They don't help you through the long developmental stages, as Kwan (2008, 2009) found in her study of PhD students trying to select readings for their theses. Or, the typical guide books make topic selection seem unproblematic. For instance, Creswell (2009, pp. 23–25), now in the fourth edition of his popular book on quantitative, qualitative, and mixed-method research design (2014), has only a couple of pages on topic development at the beginning of his chapter on literature reviews. In the prescriptive imperative style characteristic of his books, he says simply: "Before considering what literature to use in a project, first identify a topic to study and reflect on whether it is practical and useful to undertake the study" (2009, p. 23). He and others, however, rarely help novice scholars get to the stage where they can "identify a topic to study."

Creswell then goes on to suggest more helpfully that at this very early point we devise a full title for the project as a sort of cognitive organizer for the topic and then revise the title as needed. I also use titles as an organizer, sometimes at very early stages of projects, and find that titles provide me with a vision of my end product that guides me throughout the project. But the title doesn't usually come to me until my ideas for a project have already been internalized and a more or less intact vision of the whole has descended upon me. At that point, they are great guides. In contrast, unlike me, some people find that they cannot come up with a title until the very end of a project (rather like writing the introduction to the dissertation after all other chapters have been written). You will need to find a way to refine the vision of your topic in ways appropriate to your style. For instance, maybe you don't need a title but a purpose statement. Creswell equates titles with purposes statements, and there is no doubt some connection. As I mentioned in Chapter 4, playing with purpose statements is a valuable exercise from the earliest stages. But there too, we have to have some ideas already in place in order to write even the vaguest of purpose statements. Moreover, the "purpose statement" or "title" exercise needs to be revisited many times over many months. It is a useful exercise at the refinement stage. The statement can be rewritten many times. I envision a long list of either titles or purpose statements from the earliest stages in a project, a list that gets refined over time.

In this chapter, I assume that you already have some ideas about what your topic might or could be. I hope to convince you that changes and confusion are normal and that you might go through many iterations of one or more topics in the process of refining it. I'll talk about the value of pilot studies, conference presentations, and collegial consultations, of situating your project in the literature that you review, and of situating yourself as an actor in your project. These are all ways to focus and refine a topic and the methods that the topic demands. If your ideas are already crystal clear and have been approved by your adviser, if you don't expect to make changes, and if you have already done the situating work, then don't bother reading this chapter. Go out for a cup of coffee with a friend instead.

☞ The Normality of Zig-Zagging

Unless you have been handed a doctoral research topic by an adviser, zig-zagging toward your refined topic is normal. Look at what Eriko went through (Chapter 4). Mayumi Fujioka (2008), too, told of having a proposal draft done on one topic and changing both topic and adviser (Chapter 7). Read as well the story of Yongyan Li trying to find a focus for her dissertation, written at a university in Hong Kong under the British system (Li & Flowerdew, 2008). This process is not necessarily fun, but it is normal. From my own experience, I shifted radically from a topic in reading to a topic in writing (Chapter 1). Also from my experience, I recall one classmate in my doctoral program who actually got farther than I did in his proposal before making major changes (I dumped my idea before the proposal stage): His proposal was written, his committee chosen, and his proposal defense passed. But his committee, one world-renowned expert in particular, recommended so many changes that my classmate gave up, dumped the whole proposal, started over with a new but related topic, and formed a new committee, eliminating the famous expert. This is a major zig (or was it a zag?), more than most doctoral students experience. But he finished his entire project on time, six months faster than I did.

☞ The Value of Meditative Time Alone and Long Talks

Time alone seems crucial at certain stages of creative thinking. I used to get ideas for projects during long showers, but because droughts in California continue to worsen, I no longer use that method, and get in and out of the shower as quickly as I can. My water bill has gone down, along with my shower creativity. But long walks, often with book or article in hand, help me into, and through, many projects for research and writing. I cannot do this if I am walking with another person; it only works if I am alone and if I make time to walk for at least 45 minutes to an hour. The rhythm of my feet on the bike path or beach are a kind of meditation. The point is not that walking is the best method for mulling and meditating on project ideas, but that time alone, time to think, time to spin wheels is essential. If yoga works for you, or long semi-conscious naps, or extra time in bed especially in the morning hours, or time spent commuting by bus or train (which can place you in the midst of crowds yet offer paradoxical privacy), then use this precious private time for mulling. Plans can emerge, dilemmas can be resolved, direction found, small refinements discovered. I suggest carrying a small notebook or electronic device with you at all times so that in transit you can jot down ideas before they disappear into the stratosphere, especially if you are a middle-aged doctoral student, who for some bizarre reason can remember telephone numbers but not names or important ideas.

Not all creative thinking comes during periods of solitude. Long talks with a sympathetic colleague who is a good listener, and whom you can repay by being a good listener for him or her, have the advantage of providing you with instant feedback and contrasting or conforming views to yours. At the topic refinement stage, being forced to explain your project to someone—its rationale, its details, its methods and hoped-for participants, its obstacles, its concepts—go a long way toward putting your ideas into language that someone else can understand. It is a short step from this point to actual writing. Once you are ready to start refining your ideas in writing, you can also share them with a trusted colleague, who can read and respond to them at his or her leisure (see Chapter 3 on writing memos and journals). A trusted writing partner-collaborator will help you wrestle with ideas and even with actual pieces of writing (Van Cleave & Bridges-Rhoads, 2013).

The point is that at the refining stage, ideas need to get put into spoken, written, and graphic (images, models, pictures) language in whatever way suits your style and then developed with a certain amount of intensity and attention. Such techniques contribute to the activity of refining.

◠ The Value of Pilot Studies

Pilot studies serve multiple purposes, the most basic of which is to provide doctoral students with hands-on experience doing research. But the pilot study is perhaps most important in helping students learn some very concrete things about their proposed topic, research methods, participants, and relevant readings early enough so it is possible to shift directions or adjust readings or reconsider who the participants will be. In my case, described in Chapter 1, my pilot study convinced me that I had chosen the wrong topic, which I subsequently dropped altogether. I don't regret all the reading and learning I did during that year—it has all served me well over the years. If you want to read more examples (brief) of the role of pilot studies, see the stories of several of the doctoral students in Hong Kong described by Kwan (2008), who also found that their pilot studies helped them greatly to focus their readings and their research goals early in their PhD thesis projects.

Important for doctoral projects involving in-person participants is the need at this point to learn who is available to participate in your project and to begin getting commitments from them orally and eventually on a consent form. Pilot studies can help you identify participants and settings that will work, and eliminate ones that do not. At the refinement stage, getting access and permissions is essential and should not be postponed.

◠ The Value of Presenting at Conferences

Presenting one's preliminary ideas and pilot study findings at a professional conference can be terrifying the first time, but the organizing and thinking and reading required to put together a conference presentation can be very valuable at early stages of a doctoral project. The conference does not need to be an international one. It can be as local as the university or department itself. In my own doctoral program, several other doctoral students and I organized what we called a Forum, whose purpose was to allow students in our program to present some of their early doctoral work. We organized the Forums without faculty guidance in the style of a regular conference, including inviting a guest speaker, printing up programs with abstracts, and selecting proposals from the work of our peers. A more formal version of this kind of local conference takes place at one of my affiliations, the Graduate College of Education at Temple University's Japan Campus, for similar purposes—to give doctoral students a chance to present their ideas and preliminary findings and get some feedback from an interested audience. This colloquium too is run like a real conference, but this one with faculty guidance.

Larger and more prestigious domestic and international conferences offer the same benefits in terms of what it takes for students to prepare for them, but they tend to be much more selective about who will be chosen to present and the audience more expert and possibly more critical. The chance to present early stages of work, however, is invaluable at the refining stage, as is the opportunity to meet real experts in the field—to network, make contacts, and listen to other relevant presentations.

⌒ Situating a Project in the Literature

In Chapter 5 I talked a lot about reading in the early stages of a doctoral project. At the early exploratory stage, taking a broad sweep of a variety of potentially useful literatures is about the only way to start unless your adviser hands you a reading list and tells you that you don't need to look further. (This actually happens fairly often, I think.) But at the topic refinement stage, your reading needs to become much more focused on materials that are likely to feed directly into your project and end up in the reference list of your dissertation. It is not enough to continue a search using key words and electronic databases. Rather, guidance from advisers and other professors and colleagues, following leads from relevant readings already found, and focused interaction with your own evolving topic and methods characterize the literature search at this stage, what Kwan (2009) called the social and contingent dimension. An uncontroversial view is that "there is frequently a close relationship between the literature review and the various attempts at constructing and refining a problem, . . ." (Kilbourn, 2006, p. 566). Just how focused the review should be is a matter of discussion.

Although scholars agree that dissertation writers need to situate their projects in the literature, there are two views about how much and what kinds of reading are needed to do this (see Chapter 5). One view is that literature reviewing is a central element in the preparation of a doctoral dissertation and should be done throughout the course work and pre-dissertation period (Boote & Beile, 2005). Boote and Beile believe further that literature reviews should be broad and comprehensive, covering all that doctoral students can find in their areas of interest. This activity does not mean just finding and summarizing articles; rather, it refers to critically analyzing and synthesizing the views of others—a skill that cannot be learned at the last minute.

No one would argue with students' need to learn how to analyze and synthesize their readings as part of the task of situating their own projects in their fields. However, disagreements exist as to how extensive students' literature reviews should be. Maxwell (2006) disputed some of Boote and Beile's claims and argued instead that relevance, more than coverage, should be the goal of the reading that students do. In other words, students need to construct a literature review that presents an argument for why and how their own study will be carried out. As Maxwell (2006, p. 28) pointed out, the literature review should not be exhaustive, but relevant: "The key word is 'relevant'; relevant works are those that have important implications for the design, conduct, or interpretation of the study, not simply those that deal with the topic, or in the defined field or substantive area, of the research." In helping students determine what readings are relevant, Maxwell (2005, 2006, 2013) integrates the functions of a conceptual framework (see Chapter 6) and a literature review, emphasizing how they both influence the rationale, design, methods, and validity of a study. In this view, in other words, at the topic–project refinement stage, the literature review needs to be selective and contribute directly to the student's project rather than comprehensive (Krathwohl & Smith, 2005), and to be developed in conjunction with pilot studies, early data collection, and other contingencies (Kwan, 2008, 2009). However, relevant theoretical and empirical readings might be found *outside* as well as within students' disciplinary areas, particularly in the social sciences, which draw on multiple disciplines. So situating a project in the literature during the topic refinement process might need to be reconceptualized as situating it in the "literatureS."

Whichever choice you make for your literature review—the traditional comprehensive coverage or the selective relevance approach—your refined and focused project will be situated in a body of work that you need to be familiar with. The review will, ultimately, make clear why and how you are doing your particular study and show how it fits within, and builds onto, existing work. Along with information gleaned from early data collection and pilot studies, advisers and key professors can guide you in this choice of readings and may themselves have preferences about which approach to take.

☞ Situating Oneself in the Project (as Insider or Outsider)

In the write-up of your dissertation, you will either situate yourself openly as an insider, acknowledging who you are and how your choices and involvement influence your study, or as a faux-outsider, one who gazes in but remains to the extent possible a neutral observer and discoverer of facts. However, whether you confess to it in your dissertation or not, you are inextricably an insider in your project. Your role becomes clear at the refinement stage. *You* are the one who makes the decisions and does the research activities. You make and refine the design and data collection instruments, you conduct the study in certain ways and not others, you observe and make notes, your participation in interviews influences the interactions with participants, you listen to and transcribe tapes selectively and imperfectly, and you construct and interpret findings (findings do *not* emerge from data). You and the context of your project influence every aspect of your dissertation research (Maxwell, 2012; Mishler, 1986). In some kinds of qualitative inquiry, researchers are even participants in their own studies (Kusaka, 2014), "deep insiders" (Edwards, 2002; Labaree, 2002), or use themselves as objects of study, as in autoethnographies (Canagarajah, 2012; Ellis, Adams, & Bochner, 2011; Ellis & Bochner, 2000; Simon-Maeda, 2011).

It is a good idea at the topic refinement stage to decide what role you will play in your study and how you will represent yourself in your work. At the very least consult some manuals for researching and writing in the social sciences, as well as your advisers and other professors, to get a sense of where and how you belong. However, do not blindly follow advice to eliminate yourself and your voice from your study. This is an outmoded view. Even the conservative *Publication Manual of the American Psychological Association* (APA Manual) requires that you use first-person *I* (not *we* for single author and not third person—*the researcher—*

and not passive voice) to describe what you did. The stereotypical overuse of passive voice in social science research persists in some quarters, but by researchers who have not kept up with the times.

☞ Seeking Ongoing Input from Professors, Advisers, More Advanced Students, and a Trusted Writing Partner

At the topic refinement stage, just as at earlier stages, it is a good idea not to try to proceed alone. All doctoral students step into new territory as they enter the detailed phase of planning for dissertation projects, and it is almost impossible to figure out refinements to topics and methods without the help of knowledgeable others. At this stage, if you feel neglected and isolated, it is time to take action and seek help from a variety of people—compatible professors you have gotten to know, advisers or committee members, other students who have already gone through what you are going through, and, if you are lucky, a person inside or outside your department who can become a writing partner with whom you can exchange ideas and drafts (Van Cleave & Bridges-Rhoads, 2013).

The dilemma is, of course, that everyone is or seems to be too busy with their own work to help out (see Chapter 7 on advisers and mentors). Some shy students or students from educational systems in which it is considered improper for students to behave proactively with authority figures might have trouble demanding attention from professors and advisers. But remember: It is their job to help you. Most professors expect to be pestered by students periodically and official advisers expect to meet you regularly, even if they are not the ones to initiate meetings. More advanced students have no such obligations, but if you strike up friendships with a few of them, they are often willing to help out and also to share stories with you about their own topic refinement strategies. You may also find ways to reciprocate—perhaps by being a sounding board for issues in their own more advanced project work.

Isolation at the topic-project refinement stage can result in many wasted hours and in dangerous attitudes of discouragement. The point is: Reach out.

And now, dear readers, I send you on your way. Adventures await you on this journey.

Summary of Main Points in This Chapter

1. Topic refinement generally does not happen in a direct and linear way, but rather in a way that involves twists and turns.

2. Quiet time alone for reading, thinking, mulling, and decision-making is needed at the project refinement stage. At the same time, good talks with a trusted friend or colleague or even a responsive adviser can help you put your evolving ideas into words.

3. Pilot studies and presenting at conferences both contribute to topic and method refinement and can also help you determine which participants will actually be available for your research.

4. All doctoral projects are situated in some kinds of literature. Continuing to refine a literature search will be a major activity at the topic refinement stage. A traditional approach to the literature is that it must be reviewed quite comprehensively. An alternative approach is that literature should be relevant and selective.

5. No matter what kind of doctoral project you do, you have a role in all aspects of it. You will need to decide how overtly you acknowledge your own role or whether this will be hidden for the most part.

☞ Suggestions for Discussion and Reflection ☜

1. What are your strategies for thinking through problems and making decisions about the details of your dissertation project? What are the benefits to you of solitary or social thinking time?

2. What kinds of practice have you had at developing and refining your ideas by means of pilot studies or conference presentations? How have these activities helped you, and what would you recommend to others?

3. At the refinement stage of your dissertation project, what reading strategies are you using? What suggestions for reading strategies have you gotten from professors, advisers, or more advanced classmates? What problems at this stage are you having in selecting and evaluating readings that pertain to your refined topic?

4. As you refine your project, what role do you see for yourself in the actual research? In the eventual write-up of the findings?

References

Abasi, A. R., Akbari, N., & Graves, B. (2008). Academic literacy and plagiarism: Conversations with international graduate students and disciplinary professors. *Journal of English for Academic Purposes, 7*(4), 221–233.

American Psychological Association. (2009). *Publication manual of the American Psychological Association* (6th ed.). Washington, DC: APA.

Anfara, V. A., Jr., & Mertz, N. T. (Eds.). (2006). *Theoretical frameworks in qualitative research.* Thousand Oaks, CA: Sage Publications.

Atkinson, D. (2010). Between theory with a big T and practice with a small p: Why theory matters. In T. Silva & P. K. Matsuda (Eds.), *Practicing theory in second language writing* (pp. 5–18). West Lafayette, IN: Parlor Press.

Becker, H. S. (1986). *Writing for social scientists: How to start and finish your thesis, book, or article.* Chicago: University of Chicago Press.

Becker, H. S. (1998). *Tricks of the trade: How to think about your research while you're doing it.* Chicago: The University of Chicago Press.

Belcher, D. (1994). The apprenticeship approach to advanced academic literacy: Graduate students and their mentors. *English for Specific Purposes, 13,* 23–34.

Belcher, D., & Hirvela, A. (2005). Writing the qualitative dissertation: What motivates and sustains commitment to a fuzzy genre? *Journal of English for Academic Purposes, 4,* 187–205.

Berger, P., & Luckmann, T. (1966). *The social construction of reality.* Garden City, NY: Doubleday.

Billig, M. (2013). *Learn to write badly: How to succeed in the social sciences.* Cambridge, U.K.: Cambridge University Press.

Boote, D. N., & Beile, P. (2005). Scholars before researchers: On the centrality of the dissertation literature review in research preparation. *Educational Researcher, 34*(6), 3–15.

Boote, D. N., & Beile P. (2006). On "Literature reviewers of, and for, educational research": A response to the critique by Joseph Maxwell. *Educational Researcher, 35*(9), 32–35.

Cadman, K. (2000). 'Voices in the air': Evaluations of the learning experiences of international postgraduates and their supervisors. *Teaching in Higher Education, 5*(4), 475–491.

Canagarajah, A. S. (2012). Teacher development in a global profession: An autoethnography. *TESOL Quarterly, 46*(2), 258–279.

Carnell, E., MacDonald, J., McCallum, B., & Scott, M. (2008). *Passion and politics: Academics reflect on writing for publication.* London: Institute of Education.

Casanave, C. P. (1992). Cultural diversity and socialization: A case study of a Hispanic woman in a doctoral program in sociology. In D. E. Murray (Ed.), *Diversity as resource: Redefining cultural literacy* (pp. 148–182). Alexandria, VA: TESOL.

Casanave, C. P. (2002). *Writing games: Multicultural case studies of academic literacy practices in higher education.* Mahwah, NJ: Lawrence Erlbaum Associates.

Casanave, C. P. (2008). Learning participatory practices in graduate school: Some perspective-taking by a mainstream educator. In C. P. Casanave & X. Li (Eds.), *Learning the literacy practices of graduate school: Insiders' reflections on academic enculturation* (pp. 14–31). Ann Arbor: University of Michigan Press.

Casanave, C. P. (2010a). Dovetailing under impossible circumstances. In C. Aitchison, B. Kamler, & A. Lee (Eds.), *Publishing pedagogies for the doctorate and beyond* (pp. 47–63). New York: Routledge.

Casanave, C. P. (2010b). Taking risks?: A case study of three doctoral students writing qualitative dissertations at an American university in Japan. *Journal of Second Language Writing, 19*(1), 1–16.

Casanave, C. P. (2011). *Journal writing in second language education.* Ann Arbor: University of Michigan Press.

Casanave, C. P., & Li, Y. (September, 2012). Whole-person reciprocal mentoring. Paper presented at the Symposium on Second Language Writing, Purdue University, West Lafayette, IN.

Casanave, C. P., & Li, Y. (March, 2013). Novices' struggles with conceptual framing in writing papers for publication. Paper presented at the TESOL Convention, Dallas, TX.

Casanave, C. P., & Sosa, M. (2008). Getting in line: The challenge (and importance) of speaking and writing about difficult topics. In D. Belcher and A. Hirvela (Eds.), *The oral/literate connection: Perspectives on speaking, writing, and other media interactions* (pp. 87–109). Ann Arbor: University of Michigan Press.

Casanave, C. P., & Vandrick, S. (2003). Introduction: Issues in writing for publication. In C. P. Casanave & S. Vandrick (Eds.). *Writing for scholarly publication: Behind the scenes in language education* (pp. 1–13). Mahwah, NJ: Lawrence Erlbaum.

Caulley, D. N. (2008). Making qualitative research reports less boring: The techniques of writing creative nonfiction. *Qualitative Inquiry, 14*(3), 424–449.

Chang, Y-J., & Kanno, Y. (2010). NNES doctoral students in English-speaking academe: The nexus between language and discipline. *Applied Linguistics, 31*(5), 671–692.

Cole, M. (1996). *Cultural psychology: A once and future discipline.* Cambridge, MA: Harvard University Press.

Creighton, L., Creighton, T., & Parks, D. (2010). Mentoring to degree completion: Expanding the horizons of doctoral protégés. *Mentoring & Tutoring: Partnership in Learning, 18*(1), 39–52.

Creswell, J. W. (2009). *Research design: Qualitative, quantitative, and mixed methods approaches* (3rd ed.). Thousand Oaks, CA: Sage Publications.

Creswell, J. W. (2014). *Research design: Qualitative, quantitative, and mixed methods approaches* (4th ed.). Thousand Oaks, CA: Sage Publications.

Curry, M. J., & Lillis, T. (2013). *A scholar's guide to getting published in English: Critical choices and practice strategies.* Bristol, U.K.: Multilingual Matters.

Damasio, A. (1994). *Decartes' error: Emotion, reason, and the human brain.* New York: G. P. Putnam's Sons.

Damasio, A. (1999). *The feeling of what happens: Body and emotion in the making of consciousness.* New York: Harcourt Brace.

Danielewicz, J. (1999). Writing letters instead of journals in a teacher-education course. In S. Gardner & T. Fulwiler (Eds.). (1999). *The journal book: For teachers in technical and professional programs* (pp. 92–105). Portsmouth, NH: Boynton/Cook.

Delamont, S., Parry, O., & Atkinson, P. (1998). Creating a delicate balance: The doctoral supervisor's dilemmas. *Teaching in Higher Education, 3*(2), 157–173.

Denzin, N. K., & Lincoln, Y. S. (2000). Introduction: The discipline and practice of qualitative research. In N. K. Denzin & Y. S. Lincoln (Eds.), *The SAGE handbook of qualitative research* (2nd ed.) (pp. 1–28). Thousand Oaks, CA: Sage Publications.

Dong, Y. R. (1998). Non-native graduate students' thesis/dissertation writing in science: Self-reports by students and their advisors from two U.S. institutions. *English for Specific Purposes, 17*(4), 369–390.

Edwards, B. (2002). Deep insider research. *Qualitative Research Journal, 2*(1), 71–84.

Eisner, C., & Vicinus, M. (Eds.). (2008). *Originality, imitation, and plagiarism: Teaching writing in the digital age.* Ann Arbor: University of Michigan Press.

Ellis, C., Adams, T. E., & Bochner, A. P. (2011). Autoethnography: An overview (40 paragraphs). *Forum: Qualitative Social Research, 12*(1), Art. 10. www.qualitative-research.net/index.php/fqs/article/view/1589/

Ellis, C. S., & Bochner, A. (2000). Autoethnography, personal narrative, reflexivity: Researcher as subject. In N. K. Denzin & Y. S. Lincoln (Eds.), *The SAGE handbook of qualitative research* (2nd ed.) (pp. 733–768). Thousand Oaks, CA: Sage Publications.

Feak, C, B., & Swales, J. M. (2009). *Telling a research story: Writing a literature review.* Ann Arbor: University of Michigan Press.

Fleck, L. (1935/1979). *Genesis and development of a scientific fact* (F. Bradley and T. Trenn, Trans.). Chicago: University of Chicago Press.

Franke, A., & Arvidsson, B. (2008). Research supervisors' different ways of experiencing supervision of doctoral students. *Studies in Higher Education, 36*(1), 7–19.

Fujioka, M. (2008). Dissertation writing and the (re)positioning of self in a "community of practice." In C. P. Casanave & X. Li (Eds.), *Learning the literacy practices of graduate school: Insiders' reflections on academic enculturation* (pp. 58–73). Ann Arbor: University of Michigan Press.

Golde, C. (2000). Should I stay or should I go? Student descriptions of the doctoral attrition process. *Review of Higher Education 23*, 199–227.

Golde, C. M. (2005). The role of the department and discipline in doctoral student attrition: Lessons from four departments. *Journal of Higher Education, 76*(6), 669–700.

Gu, Q., & Brooks, J. (2008). Beyond the accusation of plagiarism. *System, 36*(3), 337–352.

Guba, E. G., & Lincoln, Y. S. (2005). Paragdigmatic controversies, contradictions, and emerging confluences. In N. K. Denzin & Y. S. Lincoln (Eds.), *The SAGE handbook of qualitative research* (3rd ed.) (pp. 191–215). Thousand Oaks, CA: Sage Publications.

Halse, C., & Malfroy, J. (2010). Retheorizing doctoral supervision as professional work. *Studies in Higher Education, 35*(1), 79–92.

Hasrati, M. (2005). Legitimate peripheral participation and supervising PhD students. *Studies in Higher Education, 30*(5), 557–570.

Hesse-Biber, S. (2010). Qualitative approaches to mixed methods practice. *Qualitative Inquiry, 16*(6), 455–468.

Hood, M. (in preparation). *Crossing boundaries, raising voices: A study of three Japanese graduate students in U.S. universities.* Unpublished doctoral dissertation, Temple University, Tokyo, Japan/Philadelphia, Pennsylvania.

Howard, R. M. (1995). Plagiarisms, authorships, and the academic death penalty. *College English, 57*(7), 788–806.

Ives, G., & Rowley, G. (2005). Supervisor selection or allocation and continuity of supervison: Ph.D. students' progress and outcomes. *Studies in Higher Education, 30*(5), 535–555.

Johnson, R. B., & Onwuegbuzie, A. J. (2004). Mixed methods research: A research paradigm whose time has come. *Educational Researcher, 33*(7), 14–26.

Kamler, B., & Thomson, P. (2008). The failure of dissertation advice books: Toward alternative pedagogies for doctoral writing. *Educational Researcher, 37*(8), 507–514.

Kilbourn, B. (2006). The qualitative doctoral dissertation proposal. *Teachers College Record, 108*(4), 529–576.

Kim, Y. (2007). Difficulties in quality doctoral academic advising: Experiences of Korean students. *Journal of Research in International Education, 6*(2), 171–193.

Krathwohl, D. R., & Smith, N. L. (2005). *How to prepare a dissertation proposal: Suggestions for students in education and the social and behavioral sciences.* Syracuse, NY: Syracuse University Press.

Kuhn, T. S. (1970). *The structure of scientific revolutions* (2ⁿᵈ ed.). Chicago: University of Chicago Press.

Kusaka, L. (2014). *Negotiating identities: An interview study and autoethnography of six Japanese American TESOL professionals in Japan.* Unpublished doctoral dissertation, Temple University, Tokyo, Japan/Philadelphia, Pennsylvania.

Kuwahara, N. (2008). It's not in the orientation manual: How a first-year doctoral student learned to survive in graduate school. In C. P. Casanave & X. Li (Eds.), *Learning the literacy practices of graduate school: Insiders' reflections on academic enculturation* (pp. 186–200). Ann Arbor: University of Michigan Press.

Kwan, B. S. C. (2008). The nexus of reading, writing and researching in the doctoral undertaking of humanities and social sciences: Implications for literature reviewing. *English for Specific Purposes, 27*(1), 42–56.

Kwan, B. S. C. (2009). Reading in preparation for writing a PhD thesis: Case studies of experiences. *Journal of English for Academic Purposes, 8*(3), 180–191.

Labaree, R.V. (2002). The risk of 'going observationalist': Negotiating the hidden dilemmas of being an insider participant observer. *Qualitative Research, 2*(1), 97–122.

Lantolf, J. P., & Thorne, S. L. (2006). *Sociocultural theory and the genesis of second language development.* Oxford, U.K.: Oxford University Press.

Lave, J., & Wenger, E. (1991). *Situated learning: Legitimate peripheral participation.* Cambridge, U.K.: Cambridge University Press.

Lee, A. (2007). Developing effective supervisors: Concepts of research supervision. *South African Journal of Higher Education, 21*(4), 680–693.

Lee, A. (2008). How are doctoral students supervised? Concepts of doctoral research supervision. *Studies in Higher Education, 33*(3), 267–281.

Li, S., & Seale, C. (2007). Managing criticism in PhD supervision: A qualitative case study. *Studies in Higher Edcuation, 32*(4), 511–526.

Li, Y., & Casanave, C. P. (2012). Two first-year students' strategies for writing from sources: Patchwriting or plagiarism? *Journal of Second Language Writing, 21*(2), 165–180.

Li, Y., & Flowerdew, J. (2008). Finding one's way into qualitative case studies in PhD thesis research: An interactive journey of a mentee and her mentor. In C. P. Casanave & X. Li (Eds.), *Learning the literacy practices of graduate school: Insiders' reflections on academic enculturation* (pp. 105–120). Ann Arbor: University of Michigan Press.

Lillis, T., & Curry, M. J. (2010). *Academic writing in a global context: The politics and practices of publishing in English.* London: Routledge.

Locke, L., Spirduso, W. W., & Silverman, S. J. (1999). *Proposals that work* (4th ed.). Thousand Oaks, CA: Sage Publications.

Lovitts, B.E. (2001). *Leaving the ivory tower: The causes and consequences of departure from doctoral study.* Lanham, MD: Rowman & Littlefield.

Lovitts, B. E. (2005). Being a good course-taker is not enough: A theoretical perspective on the transition to independent research. *Studies in Higher Education, 30*(2), 137–154.

Lunsford, L. (2012). Doctoral advising or mentoring? Effects on student outcomes. *Mentoring & Tutoring: Partnership in Learning, 20*(2), 251–270.

Maxwell, J. A. (2005). *Qualitative research design: An interactive approach.* (2nd ed.). Thousand Oaks, CA: Sage Publications.

Maxwell, J. A. (2006). Literature reviews of, and for, educational research: A commentary on Boote and Beile's "Scholars Before Researchers." *Educational Researcher, 35*(9), 28–31.

Maxwell, J. A. (2012). *A realist approach for qualitative research.* Thousand Oaks, CA: Sage Publications.

Maxwell, J. A. (2013). *Qualitative research design: An interactive approach* (3rd ed.). Thousand Oaks, CA: Sage Publications.

McIntosh, P. (1989). *Feeling like a fraud: Part II.* Work in Progress #37. Wellesley, MA: The Stone Center, Wellesley College.

Meloy, J. M. (1994). *Writing the qualitative dissertation: Understanding by doing.* Hillsdale, NJ: Lawrence Erlbaum.

Merton, R. K. (1967). *On theoretical sociology: Five essays old and new.* New York: Free Press.

Mishler, E. G. (1986). *Research interviewing: Context and narrative.* Cambridge, MA: Harvard University Press.

Murray, N., & Beglar, D. (2009). *Inside track: Writing dissertations and theses.* Harlow, U.K.: Pearson Education.

Noddings, N. (2003). *Caring: A feminine approach to ethics and moral education* (2nd ed.). Berkeley: University of California Press.

Ohashi, J., Ohashi, H., & Paltridge, B. (2008). Finishing the dissertation while on tenure track: Enlisting support from inside and outside the academy. In C. P. Casanave & X. Li (Eds.), *Learning the literacy practices of graduate school: Insiders' reflections on academic enculturation* (pp. 218–229). Ann Arbor: University of Michigan Press.

Okada, H. (2008). Learning to do graduate school: Learning to do life. In C. P. Casanave & X. Li (Eds.), *Learning the literacy practices of graduate school: Insiders' reflections on academic enculturation* (pp. 247–262). Ann Arbor: University of Michigan Press.

Okada, H. (2009). *Somewhere "in between": Languages and identities of three Japanese international school students.* Unpublished doctoral dissertation, Temple University, Tokyo, Japan/Philadelphia, Pennsylvania.

Paltridge, B. (2002). Thesis and dissertation writing: An examination of published advice and actual practice. *English for Specific Purposes, 21*, 125–143.

Paltridge, B., & Starfield, S. (2007). *Thesis and dissertation writing in a second language: A handbook for supervisors.* New York: Routledge.

Paltridge, B., & Woodrow, L. (2012). Thesis and dissertation writing: Moving beyond the text. In R. Tang (Ed.), *Academic writing in a second or foreign language: Issues and challenges facing ESL/EFL academic writers in higher education contexts* (pp. 88–104). London: Continuum.

Richardson, L., & St. Pierre, E. A. (2005). Writing: A method of inquiry. In N. K. Denzin & Y. S. Lincoln (Eds.), *The SAGE handbook of qualitative research* (3rd ed.) (pp. 959–978). Thousand Oaks, CA: Sage Publications.

Ridley, D. (2008). *The literature review: A step-by-step guide for students.* Thousand Oaks, CA: Sage Publications.

Silverman, D., & Marvasti, A. (2008). *Doing qualitative research: A comprehensive guide.* Thousand Oaks, CA: Sage Publications.

Simon-Maeda, A. (2011). *Being and becoming a speaker of Japanese: An autoethnographic account.* Clevedon, U.K.: Multilingual Matters.

Simpson, S., & Matsuda, P. K. (2008). Mentoring as a long-term relationship: Situated learning in a doctoral program. In C. P. Casanave & X. Li (Eds.), *Learning the literacy practices of graduate school: Insiders' reflections on academic enculturation* (pp. 90–104). Ann Arbor: University of Michigan Press.

Smagorinsky, P. (2011). *Vygotsky and literacy research: A methodological framework.* Rotterdam, The Netherlands: Sense Publishers.

Sternberg, D. (1981). *How to complete and survive a doctoral dissertation.* New York: St. Martin's Press.

Stracke, E., & Kumar, V. (2010). Feedback and self-regulated learning: Insights from supervisors' and PhD examiners' reports. *Reflective Practice, 11*(1), 19–32.

Sunstein, B. S., & Chiseri-Strater, E. (2002). *Fieldworking: Reading and writing research* (2nd ed.). New York: Bedford/St. Martin's.

Swales, J. M., and Feak, C. B. (2000). *English in today's research world: A writing guide.* Ann Arbor: University of Michigan Press.

Swales, J. M., and Feak, C. B. (2012). *Academic writing for graduate students: Essential tasks and skills* (3rd ed.). Ann Arbor: University of Michigan Press.

Swales, J. M., & Lindemann, S. (2002). Teaching the literature review to international graduate students. In A. M. Johns, (Ed.), *Genre in the classroom: Multiple perspectives* (pp. 105–119). Mahwah, NJ: Lawrence Erlbaum.

Tardy, C. (2010). Cleaning up the mess: Perspectives from a novice theory builder. In T. Silva & P. Matsuda (Eds.), *Practicing theory in second language writing* (pp. 112–125). West Lafayette, IN: Parlor Press.

Teddlie, C., & Tashakkori, A. (2009). *Foundations of mixed methods research: Integrating quantitative and qualitative approaches in the social and behavioral sciences.* Thousand Oaks, CA: Sage Publications.

Temple, B. (1997). Watch your tongue: Issues in translation and cross-cultural research. *Sociology, 31*(3), 607–618.

Temple, B., & Young, A. (2004). Qualitative research and translation dilemmas. *Qualitative Research, 4*(2), 161–178.

Thein, A. H., & Beach, R. (2010). Mentoring doctoral students towards publication within scholarly communities of practice. In C. Aitchison, B. Kamler, & A. Lee (Eds.), *Publishing pedagogies for the doctorate and beyond* (pp. 117–136). New York: Routledge.

Van Cleave, J., & Bridges-Rhoads, S. (2013). "As cited in" writing partnerships: The (im)possibility of authorship in postmodern research. *Qualitative Inquiry, 19*(9), 674–685.

Vilkinas, T. (2008). An exploratory study of the supervision of PhD/Research students' theses. *Innovative Higher Education, 32,* 297–311.

Wenger, E. (1998). *Communities of practice: Learning, meaning, and identity.* Cambridge, U.K.: Cambridge University Press.

Wertsch, J.V. (1985). *Vygotsky and the social formation of mind.* Cambridge, MA: Harvard University Press.

Wertsch, J.V. (1991). *Voices of the mind: A sociocultural approach to mediated action.* Cambridge, MA: Harvard University Press.

Wolcott, H. (2001). *Writing up qualitative research* (2nd ed.). Thousand Oaks, CA: Sage Publications.

Wolcott, H. F. (2005). *The art of fieldwork* (2nd ed.). Walnut Creek, CA: Altamira Press.

Yi, Y. (2005a). Asian adolescents' in and out-of-school encounters with English and Korean literacy. *Journal of Asian Pacific Communication, 15*(1), 57–77.

Yi, Y. (2005b). *Immigrant students' out-of-school literacy practices: A qualitative study of Korean students' experiences.* Unpublished doctoral dissertation, The Ohio State University, Columbus, Ohio.

Yi, Y. (2013). Adolescent multilingual writer's negotiation of multiple identities and access to academic writing: A case study of a *jogi yuhak* student in a U.S. high school. *The Canadian Modern Language Review, 69*(2), 207–231.

Zhao, C.-M., Golde, C. M., & McCormick, A. C. (2007). More than a signature: How advisor choice and advisor behaviour affect doctoral student satisfaction. *Journal of Further and Higher Education, 31*(3), 263–281.

Subject Index

149

Author Index

153